Modern Critical Interpretations

William Shakespeare's
The Merchant of Venice

Modern Critical Interpretations

These and other titles in preparation

Modern Critical Interpretations

William Shakespeare's
The Merchant of Venice

Edited and with an introduction by

Harold Bloom
Sterling Professor of the Humanities
Yale University

Chelsea House Publishers ◊ *1986*

NEW YORK ◊ NEW HAVEN ◊ PHILADELPHIA

©1986 by Chelsea House Publishers, a division of
Chelsea House Educational Communications, Inc.
133 Christopher Street, New York, NY 10014
345 Whitney Avenue, New Haven, CT 06511
5014 West Chester Pike, Edgemont, PA 19028

Introduction © 1986 by Harold Bloom

Printed and bound in the United States of America

∞The paper used in this publication meets the minimum requirements of
the American National Standard for Permanence of Paper for Printed Library
Materials, Z39.48–1984.

Library of Congress Cataloging-in-Publication Data   *142 p'*
William Shakespeare — The merchant of Venice.
(Modern critical interpretations)
Bibliography: p.*133 - 134*
Includes index.
1. Shakespeare, William, 1564–1616. Merchant of
Venice — Addresses, essays, lectures. I. Bloom, Harold.
II. Series.
PR2825.W55   1986   822.3'3   86-2581
ISBN 0-87754-932-X (alk. paper)

Contents

Editor's Note

This book gathers together what seems to me the most stimulating criticism of our century upon Shakespeare's *The Merchant of Venice*. I am grateful to Marena Fisher for her erudition and judgment in helping me to find and select these essays.

The introduction contrasts Shakespeare's Shylock to Marlowe's Barabas (in *The Jew of Malta*) and seeks to account for what I consider Shakespeare's unwonted lack of originality in his representation of the Jew as compared to Marlowe's, despite the surface "humanization" of Shylock when contrasted to Barabas, the hero-villain of what professes to be bloody farce.

Freud's famous paper of 1913 on the theme of the three caskets begins the chronological sequence, which continues with E. E. Stoll's deeply informed historical view of Shylock. In contradistinction to Stoll, Harold C. Goddard attempts to rescue Shakespeare from his palpable anti-Semitism by arguing that the play depicts Portia as being untrue to herself. This moving idealization is set aside in C. L. Barber's account of Shylock as the alien intruder in the festive communion of a comedy of wealth.

Leslie A. Fiedler, both a Freudian with a difference, and a Marxist, like myself more of Groucho's than of Karl's persuasion, argues intricately for a reading in which the play becomes essentially a sexual struggle for Bassanio between Portia and Antonio. In this reading, the Jew becomes an opponent of the pleasure principle. Equally extreme, but in a very different direction, is the characteristic analysis of René Girard, by which Shylock is the ritual scapegoat in a Shakespearean irony that has entrapped the wisest readers.

This book concludes with two younger critics applying the intricacies of current advanced modes of rhetorical criticism to what I suspect was not problematic for Shakespeare, yet is for us. Marc Shell explores metaphors of economy and of "verbal usury," while Jerome Christensen concentrates upon Coleridge's treatment of a single nautical metaphor in the play. What emerges from both critics is the figurative equivalent of the paradoxical separation between force and farce that the other critics have discussed more thematically.

Introduction

Shylock is to the world of the comedies and romances what Hamlet is to the tragedies, and Falstaff to the histories: a representation so original as to be perpetually bewildering to us. What is beyond us in Hamlet and Falstaff is a mode of vast consciousness crossed by wit, so that we know authentic disinterestedness only by knowing the Hamlet of act 5, and know the wit that enlarges existence best by knowing Falstaff before his rejection by King Henry V, who has replaced Hal. Shylock is not beyond us in any way, and yet he resembles Hamlet and Falstaff in one crucial regard: he is a much more problematical representation than even Shakespeare's art could have intended. Like Hamlet and Falstaff, he dwarfs his fellow characters. Portia, despite her aura, fades before him just as Claudius recedes in the clash of mighty opposites with Hamlet, and as Hotspur is dimmed by Falstaff.

I know of no legitimate way in which *The Merchant of Venice* ought to be regarded as other than an anti-Semitic text, agreeing in this with E. E. Stoll as against Harold Goddard, my favorite critic of Shakespeare. Goddard sees Antonio and Portia as self-betrayers, who should have done better. They seem to me perfectly adequate Christians, with Antonio's anti-Semitism being rather less judicious than Portia's, whose attitude approximates that of the T. S. Eliot of *After Strange Gods, The Idea of a Christian Society*, and the earlier poems. If you accept the attitude towards the Jews of the Gospel of John, then you will behave towards Shylock as Portia does, or as Eliot doubtless would have behaved towards British Jewry, had the Nazis defeated and occupied Eliot's adopted country. To Portia, and to Eliot, the Jews were what they are called in the Gospel of John: descendants of Satan, rather than of Abraham.

There is no real reason to doubt that the historical Shakespeare would have agreed with his Portia. Shakespeare after all wrote what might as well be called *The Jew of Venice*, in clear rivalry with his precursor Marlowe's *The Jew of Malta*. Were I an actor, I would take great pleasure in the part of Barabas, and little

1

or none in that of Shylock, but then I am a Jewish critic, and prefer the exuberance of Barabas to the wounded intensity of Shylock. There is nothing problematic about Barabas. We cannot imagine *him* asking: "If you prick us, do we not bleed?," anymore than we can imagine Shylock proclaiming: "As for myself, I walk abroad a-nights . . . and poison wells." Marlowe, subtly blasphemous and cunningly outrageous, gives us Christians and Muslims who are as reprehensible as Barabas, but who lack the Jew of Malta's superb delight in his own sublime villainy. Despite his moralizing scholars, Marlowe the poet is Barabas, or rhetorically so akin to his creation as to render the difference uninteresting. Shakespeare possibly intended to give us a pathetic monster in Shylock, but being Shakespeare, he gave us Shylock, concerning whom little can be said that will not be at least oxymoronic, if not indeed self-contradictory.

That Shylock got away from Shakespeare seems clear enough, but that is the scandal of Shakespearean representation; so strong is it that nearly all his creatures break out of the temporal trap of Elizabethan and Jacobean mimesis, and establish standards of imitation that do seem to be, not of an age, but for all time. Shylock also—like Hamlet, Falstaff, Cleopatra—compels us to see differences in reality we otherwise could not have seen. Marlowe is a great caricaturist; Barabas is grotesquely magnificent, and his extravagance mocks the Christian cartoon of the Jew as usurer and fiend. It hardly matters whether the mockery is involuntary, since inevitably the hyperbolic force of the Marlovian rhetoric raises word-consciousness to a level where everything joins in an overreaching. In a cosmos where all is excessive, Barabas is no more a Jew than Tamburlaine is a Scythian or Faustus a Christian. It is much more troublesome to ask: Is Shylock a Jew? Does he not now represent something our culture regards as being essentially Jewish? So immense is the power of Shakespearean mimesis that its capacity for harm necessarily might be as substantial as its enabling force has been for augmenting cognition and for fostering psychoanalysis, despite all Freud's anxious assertions of his own originality.

II

Harold Goddard, nobly creating a Shakespeare in his own highly humane image, tried to persuade himself "that Shakespeare planned his play from the outset to enforce the irony of Portia's failure to be true to her inner self in the trial scene." E. E. Stoll, sensibly declaring that Shakespeare's contemporary audience set societal limits that Shakespeare himself would not have thought to transcend, reminds us that Jew-baiting was in effect little different from bear-baiting for that audience. I do not hope for a better critic of Shakespeare than Goddard. Like Freud, Goddard always looked for what Shakespeare shared with Dostoevsky, which seems to me rather more useful than searching for what Shakespeare shared with Kyd or even with Marlowe or Webster. Despite his authentic insistence that Shakespeare always was poet as well as playwright, Goddard's attempt to see *The Merchant of Venice* as other than anti-Semitic was misguided.

At his very best, Goddard antithetically demonstrates that the play's "spiritual argument" is quite simply unacceptable to us now:

> Shylock's conviction that Christianity and revenge are synonyms is confirmed. "If a Christian wrong a Jew, what should his sufferance be by Christian example? Why, revenge." The unforgettable speech from which that comes, together with Portia's on mercy, and Lorenzo's on the harmony of heaven, make up the spiritual argument of the play. Shylock asserts that a Jew is a man. Portia declares that man's duty to man is mercy—which comes from heaven. Lorenzo points to heaven but laments that the materialism of life insulates man from its harmonies. A celestial syllogism that puts to shame the logic of the courtroom.

Alas, the celestial syllogism is Goddard's, and Portia's logic is Shakespeare's. Goddard wanted to associate *The Merchant of Venice* with Chekhov's bittersweet "Rothschild's Fiddle," but Dostoevsky again would have been the right comparison. Shakespeare's indubitable anti-Semitism is no lovelier than Dostoevsky's, being compounded similarly out of xenophobia and The Gospel of John. Shylock's demand for justice, as contrasted to Portia's supposed mercy, is part of the endless consequence of the New Testament's slander against the Pharisees. But the authors of the New Testament, even Paul and John, were no match for the authors of the Hebrew Bible. Shakespeare, more even than Dostoevsky, is of another order, the order of the Yahwist, Homer, Dante, Chaucer, Cervantes, Tolstoy—the great masters of Western literary representation. Shylock is essentially a comic representation rendered something other than comic because of Shakespeare's preternatural ability to accomplish a super-mimesis of essential nature. Shakespeare's intellectual, Hamlet, is necessarily the paradigm of *the* intellectual, even as Falstaff is the model of wit, and Cleopatra the sublime of eros. Is Shakespeare's Jew fated to go on being the representation of *the* Jew?

"Yes and no," would be my answer, because of Shakespeare's own partial failure when he allows Shylock to invoke an even stronger representation of *the* Jew, the Yahwist's vision of the superbly tenacious Jacob tending the flocks of Laban and not directly taking interest. Something very odd is at work when Antonio denies Jacob's own efficacy:

> This was a venture, sir, that Jacob serv'd for;
> A thing not in his power to bring to pass,
> But sway'd and fashion'd by the hand of heaven.

That is certainly a Christian reading, though I do not assert necessarily it was Shakespeare's own. Good Christian merchant that he is, Antonio distinguishes his own profits from Shylock's Jewish usury, but Shylock, or rather the Yahwist, surely wins the point over Antonio, and perhaps over Shakespeare. If the Jewish "devil can cite Scripture for his purpose," so can the Christian devils, from John through Shakespeare, and the polemical point turns upon who wins the agon, the Yahwist or Shakespeare? Shakespeare certainly intended to show the Jew as caught in the repetition of a revenge morality masking itself as a demand for justice. That is the rhetorical force of Shylock's obsessive "I will have my bond," with all its dreadfully compulsive ironic plays upon "bond." But if Shylock, like the Yahwist's Jacob, is a strong representation of the Jew, then "bond" has a tenacity that Shakespeare himself may have underestimated. Shakespeare's most dubious irony, as little persuasive as the resolution of *Measure for Measure*, is that Portia triumphantly out-literalizes Shylock's literalism, since flesh cannot be separated from blood. But Shylock, however monstrously, has a true bond or covenant to assert, whether between himself and Antonio, or between Jacob and Laban, or ultimately between Israel and Yahweh. Portia invokes an unequal law, not a covenant or mutual obligation, but only another variant upon the age-old Christian insistence that Christians may shed Jewish blood, but never the reverse. Can it be said that we do not go on hearing Shylock's "I will have my bond," despite his forced conversion?

III

Shakespearean representation presents us with many perplexities throughout the comedies and romances: Angelo and Malvolio, among others, are perhaps as baffling as Shylock. What makes Shylock different may be a strength in the language he speaks that works against what elsewhere is Shakespeare's most original power. Shylock does not change by listening to himself speaking; he becomes only more what he always was. It is as though the Jew alone, in Shakespeare, lacks originality. Marlowe's Barabas *sounds* less original than Shylock does, and yet Marlowe employs Barabas to satirize Christian moral pretensions. The curious result is that Marlowe, just this once, seems "modern" in contrast to Shakespeare. What are we to do with Shylock's great outbursts of pathos when the play itself seems to give them no dignity or value in context? I do not find it possible to contravene E. E. Stoll's judgment in this regard:

> Shylock's disappointment is tragic to him, but good care is taken
> that it shall not be to us . . . The running fire assails him to the
> very moment — and beyond it — that Shylock says he is not well, and
> staggers out, amid Gratiano's jeers touching his baptism, to provoke

in the audience the laughter of triumph and vengeance in his own day and bring tears to their eyes in ours. How can we here for a moment sympathize with Shylock unless at the same time we indignantly turn, not only against Gratiano, but against Portia, the Duke, and all Venice as well?

We cannot, unless we desire to read or see some other play. *The Merchant of Venice* demands what we cannot accept: Antonio's superior goodness, from the start, is to be demonstrated by his righteous scorn for Shylock, which is to say, Antonio most certainly represents what now is called a Jew-baiter. An honest production of the play, sensitive to its values, would now be intolerable in a Western country. The unhappy paradox is that *The Jew of Malta*, a ferocious farce, exposes the madness and hypocrisy of Jew-baiting, even though its Machiavel, Barabas, is the Jewish monster or Devil incarnate, while *The Merchant of Venice* is at once a comedy of delightful sophistication and a vicious Christian slander against the Jews.

In that one respect, Shakespeare was of an age, and not for all time. Bardolatry is not always an innocent disease, and produces odd judgments, as when J. Middleton Murry insisted: "*The Merchant of Venice* is not a problem play; it is a fairy story." For us, contemporary Jews and Gentiles alike, it had better be a problem play, and not a fairy story. Shylock, Murry admitted, was not "coherent," because a Shakespearean character had no need to be coherent. Yet Shylock is anything but incoherent. His palpable mimetic force enhances his rapacity and viciousness, and works to make an ancient bogeyman come dreadfully alive. For the reader or playgoer (though hardly the latter, in our time), Shylock is at once comic and frightening, a walking embodiment of the death drive.

We must not underestimate the power and influence of Shakespearean mimesis, even when it is *deliberately* unoriginal, as it is in Shylock. Hamlet and Falstaff contain us to our enrichment. Shylock has the strength to contain us to our destruction. Something of the same could be said for Angelo, in *Measure for Measure*, or of Malvolio, in *Twelfth Night*, or of nearly everyone in *Troilus*. History renders Shylock's strength as representation socially destructive, whereas Angelo and Malvolio inhabit the shadows of the individual consciousness. I conclude by noting that Shakespeare's comedies and romances share in the paradox that Gershom Scholem said the writings of Kafka possessed. They have for us "something of the strong light of the canonical, of the perfection that destroys."

The Theme of the Three Caskets

Sigmund Freud

Two scenes from Shakespeare, one from a comedy and the other from a tragedy, have lately given me occasion for posing and solving a small problem.

The first of these scenes is the suitors' choice between the three caskets in *The Merchant of Venice*. The fair and wise Portia is bound at her father's bidding to take as her husband only that one of her suitors who chooses the right casket from among the three before him. The three caskets are of gold, silver, and lead: the right casket is the one that contains her portrait. Two suitors have already departed unsuccessful: they have chosen gold and silver. Bassanio, the third, decides in favour of lead; thereby he wins the bride, whose affection was already his before the trial of fortune. Each of the suitors gives reasons for his choice in a speech in which he praises the metal he prefers and depreciates the other two. The most difficult task thus falls to the share of the fortunate third suitor; what he finds to say in glorification of lead as against gold and silver is little and has a forced ring. If in psycho-analytic practice we were confronted with such a speech, we should suspect that there were concealed motives behind the unsatisfying reasons produced.

Shakespeare did not himself invent this oracle of the choice of a casket; he took it from a tale in the *Gesta Romanorum*, in which a girl has to make the same choice to win the Emperor's son. Here too the third metal, lead, is the bringer of fortune. It is not hard to guess that we have here an ancient theme, which requires to be interpreted, accounted for and traced back to its origin. A first conjecture as to the meaning of this choice between gold, silver, and

From *The Standard Edition of the Complete Psychological Works of Sigmund Freud* 12 (1911–1913). © 1958 by The Institute of Psycho-analysis and Mrs. Alix Strachey. The Hogarth Press and The Institute of Psycho-Analysis, 1913.

lead is quickly confirmed by a statement of Stucken's, who has made a study of the same material over a wide field. He writes: "The identity of Portia's three suitors is clear from their choice: the Prince of Morocco chooses the gold casket — he is the sun; the Prince of Arragon chooses the silver casket — he is the moon; Bassanio chooses the leaden casket — he is the star youth." In support of this explanation he cites an episode from the Estonian folk-epic "Kalewipoeg," in which the three suitors appear undisguisedly as the sun, moon, and star youths (the last being "the Pole-star's eldest boy") and once again the bride falls to the lot of the third.

Thus our little problem has led us to an astral myth! The only pity is that with this explanation we are not at the end of the matter. The question is not exhausted, for we do not share the belief of some investigators that myths were read in the heavens and brought down to earth; we are more inclined to judge with Otto Rank that they were projected on to the heavens after having arisen elsewhere under purely human conditions. It is in this human content that our interest lies.

Let us look once more at our material. In the Estonian epic, just as in the tale from the *Gesta Romanorum*, the subject is a girl choosing between three suitors; in the scene from *The Merchant of Venice* the subject is apparently the same, but at the same time something appears in it that is in the nature of an inversion of the theme: a *man* chooses between three — caskets. If what we were concerned with were a dream, it would occur to us at once that caskets are also women, symbols of what is essential in woman, and therefore of a woman herself — like coffers, boxes, cases, baskets, and so on. If we boldly assume that there are symbolic substitutions of the same kind in myths as well, then the casket scene in *The Merchant of Venice* really becomes the inversion we suspected. With a wave of the wand, as though we were in a fairy tale, we have stripped the astral garment from our theme; and now we see that the theme is a human one, *a man's choice between three women*.

This same content, however, is to be found in another scene of Shakespeare's, in one of his most powerfully moving dramas; not the choice of a bride this time, yet linked by many hidden similarities to the choice of the casket in *The Merchant of Venice*. The old King Lear resolves to divide his kingdom while he is still alive among his three daughters, in proportion to the amount of love that each of them expresses for him. The two elder ones, Goneril and Regan, exhaust themselves in asseverations and laudations of their love for him; the third, Cordelia, refuses to do so. He should have recognized the unassuming, speechless love of his third daughter and rewarded it, but he does not recognize it. He disowns Cordelia, and divides the kingdom between the other two, to his own and the general ruin. Is not this once more the scene of a choice between three women, of whom the youngest is the best, the most excellent one?

There will at once occur to us other scenes from myths, fairy tales and literature, with the same situation as their content. The shepherd Paris has to choose between three goddesses, of whom he declares the third to be the most beautiful. Cinderella, again, is a youngest daughter, who is preferred by the prince to her two elder sisters. Psyche, in Apuleius's story, is the youngest and fairest of three sisters. Psyche is, on the one hand, revered as Aphrodite in human form; on the other, she is treated by that goddess as Cinderella was treated by her stepmother and is set the task of sorting a heap of mixed seeds, which she accomplishes with the help of small creatures (doves in the case of Cinderella, ants in the case of Psyche). Anyone who cared to make a wider survey of the material would undoubtedly discover other versions of the same theme preserving the same essential features.

Let us be content with Cordelia, Aphrodite, Cinderella and Psyche. In all the stories the three women, of whom the third is the most excellent one, must surely be regarded as in some way alike if they are represented as sisters. (We must not be led astray by the fact that Lear's choice is between three *daughters*; this may mean nothing more than that he has to be represented as an old man. An old man cannot very well choose between three women in any other way. Thus they become his daughters.)

But who are these three sisters and why must the choice fall on the third? If we could answer this question, we should be in possession of the interpretation we are seeking. We have once already made use of an application of psycho-analytic technique, when we explained the three caskets symbolically as three women. If we have the courage to proceed in the same way, we shall be setting foot on a path which will lead us first to something unexpected and incomprehensible, but which will perhaps, by a devious route, bring us to a goal.

It must strike us that this excellent third woman has in several instances certain peculiar qualities besides her beauty. They are qualities that seem to be tending towards some kind of unity; we must certainly not expect to find them equally well marked in every example. Cordelia makes herself unrecognizable, inconspicuous like lead, she remains dumb, she "loves and is silent." Cinderella hides so that she cannot be found. We may perhaps be allowed to equate concealment and dumbness. These would of course be only two instances out of the five we have picked out. But there is an intimation of the same thing to be found, curiously enough, in two other cases. We have decided to compare Cordelia, with her obstinate refusal, to lead. In Bassanio's short speech while he is choosing the casket, he says of lead (without in any way leading up to the remark):

"Thy paleness moves me more than eloquence."
("Plainness" according to another reading.)

That is to say: "Thy plainness moves me more than the blatant nature of the other two." Gold and silver are "loud"; lead is dumb—in fact like Cordelia, who "loves and is silent."

In the ancient Greek accounts of the Judgement of Paris, nothing is said of any such reticence on the part of Aphrodite. Each of the three goddesses speaks to the youth and tries to win him by promises. But, oddly enough, in a quite modern handling of the same scene this characteristic of the third one which has struck us makes its appearance again. In the libretto of Offenbach's *La Belle Hélène,* Paris, after telling of the solicitations of the other two goddesses, describes Aphrodite's behaviour in this competition for the beauty-prize:

> La troisième, ah! la troisième...
> La troisième ne dit rien.
> Elle eut le prix tout de même...

(Literally: "The third one, ah! the third one . . . the third one said nothing. She won the prize all the same."—The quotation is from Act I, scene 7, of Meilhac and Halévy's libretto. In the German version used by Freud "the third one" "*blieb stumm*"—"remained dumb.")

If we decide to regard the peculiarities of our "third one" as concentrated in her "dumbness," then psycho-analysis will tell us that in dreams dumbness is a common representation of death.

More than ten years ago a highly intelligent man told me a dream which he wanted to use as evidence of the telepathic nature of dreams. In it he saw an absent friend from whom he had received no news for a very long time, and reproached him energetically for his silence. The friend made no reply. It afterwards turned out that he had met his death by suicide at about the time of the dream. Let us leave the problem of telepathy on one side: there seems, however, not to be any doubt that here the dumbness in the dream represented death. Hiding and being unfindable—a thing which confronts the prince in the fairy tale of Cinderella three times, is another unmistakable symbol of death in dreams; so, too, is a marked pallor, of which the "paleness" of the lead in one reading of Shakespeare's text is a reminder. It would be very much easier for us to transpose these interpretations from the language of dreams to the mode of expression used in the myth that is now under consideration if we could make it seem probable that dumbness must be interpreted as a sign of being dead in productions other than dreams.

At this point I will single out the ninth story in Grimm's *Fairy Tales,* which bears the title "The Twelve Brothers." A king and a queen have twelve children, all boys. The king declares that if the thirteenth child is a girl, the boys will have to die. In expectation of her birth he has twelve coffins made. With their mother's help the twelve sons take refuge in a hidden wood, and swear death to any girl they may meet. A girl is born, grows up, and learns one day from her mother that she has had twelve brothers. She decides to seek them out, and in the wood she finds the youngest; he recognizes her, but is anxious to hide her on account of the brothers' oath. The sister says: "I will gladly die, if by so doing I can save my twelve brothers." The brothers welcome her affectionately, however, and she stays with them and looks after their house for them. In a little garden beside the house grow twelve lilies. The girl picks them and gives one to each brother. At that moment the brothers are changed into ravens, and disappear, together with the house and garden. (Ravens are spirit-birds; the killing of the twelve brothers by their sister is represented by the picking of the flowers, just as it is at the beginning of the story by the coffins and the disappearance of the brothers.) The girl, who is once more ready to save her brothers from death, is now told that as a condition she must be dumb for seven years, and not speak a single word. She submits to the test, which brings her herself into mortal danger. She herself, that is, dies for her brothers, as she promised to do before she met them. By remaining dumb she succeeds at last in setting the ravens free.

In the story of "The Six Swans" the brothers who are changed into birds are set free in exactly the same way — they are restored to life by their sister's dumbness. The girl has made a firm resolve to free her brothers, "even if it should cost her her life"; and once again (being the wife of the king) she risks her own life because she refuses to give up her dumbness in order to defend herself against evil accusations.

It would certainly be possible to collect further evidence from fairy tales that dumbness is to be understood as representing death. These indications would lead us to conclude that the third one of the sisters between whom the choice is made is a dead woman. But she may be something else as well — namely, Death itself, the Goddess of Death. Thanks to a displacement that is far from infrequent, the qualities that a deity imparts to men are ascribed to the deity himself. Such a displacement will surprise us least of all in relation to the Goddess of Death, since in modern versions and representations, which these stories would thus be forestalling, Death itself is nothing other than a dead man.

But if the third of the sisters is the Goddess of Death, the sisters are known to us. They are the Fates, the Moerae, the Parcae or the Norns, the third of whom is called Atropos, the inexorable.

We will for the time being put aside the task of inserting the interpretation that we have found into our myth, and listen to what the mythologists have to teach us about the role and origin of the Fates. (What follows is taken from Roscher's lexicon [1884–1937], under the relevant headings.)

The earliest Greek mythology (in Homer) only knew a single Μοῖρα, personifying inevitable fate. The further development of this one Moera into a company of three (or less often two) sister-goddesses probably came about on the basis of other divine figures to which the Moerae were closely related — the Graces and the Horae (the Seasons).

The Horae were originally goddesses of the waters of the sky, dispensing rain and dew, and of the clouds from which rain falls; and, since the clouds were conceived of as something that has been spun, it came about that these goddesses were looked upon as spinners, an attribute that then became attached to the Moerae. In the sun-favoured Mediterranean lands it is the rain on which the fertility of the soil depends, and thus the Horae became vegetation goddesses. The beauty of flowers and the abundance of fruit was their doing, and they were accredited with a wealth of agreeable and charming traits. They became the divine representatives of the Seasons, and it is possibly owing to this connection that there were three of them, if the sacred nature of the number three is not a sufficient explanation. For the peoples of antiquity at first distinguished only three seasons: winter, spring, and summer. Autumn was only added in late Graeco-Roman times, after which the Horae were often represented in art as four in number.

The Horae retained their relation to time. Later they presided over the times of day, as they did at first over the times of the year; and at last their name came to be merely a designation of the hours (heure, ora). The Norns of German mythology are akin to the Horae and the Moerae and exhibit this time-signification in their names. (Their names may be rendered: "What was," "What is," "What shall be.") It was inevitable, however, that a deeper view should come to be taken of the essential nature of these deities, and that their essence should be transposed on to the regularity with which the seasons change. The Horae thus became the guardians of natural law and of the divine Order which causes the same thing to recur in Nature in an unalterable sequence.

This discovery of Nature reacted on the conception of human life. The nature-myth changed into a human myth: the weather-goddesses became goddesses of Fate. But this aspect of the Horae found expression only in the Moerae, who watch over the necessary ordering of human life as inexorably as do the Horae over the regular order of nature. The ineluctable severity of Law and its relation to death and dissolution, which had been avoided in the charming figures of the Horae, were now stamped upon the Moerae, as though men had only perceived the full seriousness of natural law when they had to submit their own selves to it.

The names of the three spinners, too, have been significantly explained by mythologists. Lachesis, the name of the second, seems to denote "the accidental that is included in the regularity of destiny"—or, as we should say, "experience"; just as Atropos stands for "the ineluctable"—Death. Clotho would then be left to mean the innate disposition with its fateful implications.

But now it is time to return to the theme which we are trying to interpret— the theme of the choice between three sisters. We shall be deeply disappointed to discover how unintelligible the situations under review become and what contradictions of their apparent content result, if we apply to them the inter-pretation that we have found. On our supposition, the third of the sisters is the Goddess of Death, Death itself. But in the Judgement of Paris she is the Goddess of Love, in the tale of Apuleius she is someone comparable to the god-dess for her beauty, in *The Merchant of Venice* she is the fairest and wisest of women, in *King Lear* she is the one loyal daughter. We may ask whether there can be a more complete contradiction. Perhaps, improbable though it may seem, there is a still more complete one lying close at hand. Indeed, there certainly is; since, whenever our theme occurs, the choice between the women is free, and yet it falls on death. For, after all, no one chooses death, and it is only by a fatality that one falls a victim to it.

However, contradictions of a certain kind—replacements by the precise opposite—offer no serious difficulty to the work of analytic interpretation. We shall not appeal here to the fact that contraries are so often represented by one and the same element in the modes of expression used by the unconscious, as for instance in dreams. But we shall remember that there are motive forces in mental life which bring about replacement by the opposite in the form of what is known as reaction-formation; and it is precisely in the revelation of such hid-den forces as these that we look for the reward of this enquiry. The Moerae were created as a result of a discovery that warned man that he too is a part of nature, and, therefore, subject to the immutable law of death. Something in man was bound to struggle against this subjection, for it is only with ex-treme unwillingness that he gives up his claim to an exceptional position. Man, as we know, makes use of his imaginative activity in order to satisfy the wishes that reality does not satisfy. So his imagination rebelled against the recognition of the truth embodied in the myth of the Moerae, and constructed instead the myth derived from it, in which the Goddess of Death was replaced by the God-dess of Love and by what was equivalent to her in human shape. The third of the sisters was no longer Death; she was the fairest, best, most desirable, and most lovable of women. Nor was this substitution in any way technically diffi-cult: it was prepared for by an ancient ambivalence, it was carried out along a primaeval line of connection which could not long have been forgotten. The Goddess of Love herself, who now took the place of the Goddess of Death, had once been identical with her. Even the Greek Aphrodite had not wholly relinquished her connection with the underworld, although she had long surrendered her chthonic role to other divine figures, to Persephone, or to the triform Artemis-Hecate. The great Mother-goddesses of the oriental peoples, however, all seem to have been both creators and destroyers—both goddesses of life and fertility and goddesses of death. Thus the replacement by a wishful opposite in our theme harks back to a primaeval identity.

The same consideration answers the question how the feature of a choice came into the myth of the three sisters. Here again there has been a wishful reversal. Choice stands in the place of necessity, of destiny. In this way man overcomes death, which he has recognized intellectually. No greater triumph of wish fulfilment is conceivable. A choice is made where in reality there is obedience to a compulsion; and what is chosen is not a figure of terror, but the fairest and most desirable of women.

On closer inspection we observe, to be sure, that the original myth is not so thoroughly distorted that traces of it do not show through and betray its presence. The free choice between the three sisters is, properly speaking, no free choice, for it must necessarily fall on the third if every kind of evil is not to come about, as it does in *King Lear*. The fairest and best of women, who has taken the place of the Death-goddess, has kept certain characteristics that border on the uncanny, so that from them we have been able to guess at what lies beneath.

Shylock

E. E. Stoll

To get at Shakespeare's intention (after a fashion) is, after all, not hard. As with popular drama, great or small, he who runs may read—he who yawns and scuffles in the pit may understand. The time is past for speaking of Shakespeare as utterly impartial or inscrutable: the study of his work and that of his fellows as an expression of Elizabethan ideas and technique is teaching us better. The puzzle whether the *Merchant of Venice* is not meant for tragedy, for instance, is cleared up when, as Professor Baker suggests, we forget Sir Henry Irving's acting, and remember that the title—and the hero—is not the *Jew of Venice* as he would lead us to suppose; that this comedy is only like others, as *Measure for Measure* and *Much Ado*, not clear of the shadow of the fear of death; and that in closing with an act where Shylock and his knife are forgotten in the unravelling of the mystery between the lovers and the crowning of Antonio's happiness in theirs, it does not, from the Elizabethan point of view, perpetrate an anticlimax, but, like many another Elizabethan play, carries to completion what is a story for story's sake. "Shylock is, and always has been the hero," says Professor Schelling. But why, then, did Shakespeare drop his hero out of the play for good before the fourth act was over? It is a trick which he never repeated—a trick, I am persuaded, of which he was not capable.

Hero or not, Shylock is given a villain's due. His is the heaviest penalty to be found in all the pound of flesh stories, including that in *Il Pecorone*, which served as model for the play. Not in the Servian, the Persian, the African version, or even that of the *Cursor Mundi*, does the moneylender suffer like Shylock— impoverishment, sentence of death, and an outrage done to his faith from which

From *Shakespeare Studies: Historical and Comparative in Method.* © 1927 by Macmillan Company, © 1941 by E. E. Stoll.

Jews were guarded even by decrees of German emperors and Roman pontiffs. It was in the old play, perhaps, source of the present one; but that Shakespeare retained it shows his indifference, at least, to the amenities, as regards either Jews or Judaism. In not a single heart do Shylock's griefs excite commiseration; indeed, as they press upon him they are barbed with gibes and jeers. Coriolanus is unfortunate and at fault, but we know that the poet is with him. We know that the poet is not with Shylock, for on that point, in this play as in every other, the impartial, inscrutable poet leaves little or nothing to suggestion or surmise. As is his custom elsewhere, by the comments of the good characters, by the methods pursued in the disposition of scenes, and by the downright avowals of soliloquy, he constantly sets us right.

As for the first of these artifices, all the people who come in contact with Shylock except Tubal — among them being those of his own house, his servant and his daughter — have a word or two to say on the subject of his character, and never a good one. And in the same breath they spend on Bassanio and Antonio, his enemies, nothing but words of praise. Praise or blame, moreover, is, after Shakespeare's fashion, usually in the nick of time to guide the hearer's judgment. Lest at his first appearance the Jew should make too favourable an impression by his Scripture quotations, Antonio is led to observe that the devil can cite Scripture for his purpose; lest the Jew's motive in foregoing interest (for once in his life) should seem like the kindness Antonio takes it to be, Bassanio avows that he likes not fair terms and a villain's mind; and once the Jew has caught the Christian on the hip, every one, from Duke to Gaoler, has words of horror or detestation for him and of compassion for his victim.

As for the second artifice, the ordering of the scenes is such as to enforce this contrast. First impressions, every playwright knows (and no one better than Shakespeare himself), are momentous, particularly for the purpose of ridicule. Launcelot and Jessica, in separate scenes, are introduced before Shylock reaches home, that, hearing their story, we may side with them, and, when the old curmudgeon appears, may be moved to laughter as he complains of Launcelot's gormandizing, sleeping, and rending apparel out, and as he is made game of by the young conspirators to his face. Here, as Mr Poel has noticed, when there might be some danger of our sympathy becoming enlisted on Shylock's side because he is about to lose his daughter and some of his property, Shakespeare forestalls it. He lets Shylock, in his hesitation whether to go to the feast, take warning from a dream, but nevertheless, though he knows that they bid him not for love, decide to go in hate, in order to feed upon the prodigal Christian. And he lets him give up Launcelot, whom he has half a liking for, save that he is a huge feeder, to Bassanio — "to one that I would have him help to waste his borrowed purse." Small credit these sentiments do him; little do they add to his pathos or dignity. Still more conspicuous is this care when Shylock laments over his daughter and his ducats. Lest then by any chance a stupid or tenderhearted audience should not laugh but grieve, Salerio reports his outcries — in part word for word — two scenes in advance, as matter of mirth to himself and all the boys in Venice. It is exactly the same method as that employed in *Twelfth Night*, act 3, scene 2, where Maria comes and tells not only Sir Toby, Sir Andrew, and Fabian, but, above all, the audience, how ridiculously Malvolio is acting, before they see it for themselves. The art of the theatre, but particularly the art of the comic theatre, is the art of preparations, else it is not securely comic. But the impression first of all imparted to us is of Shylock's villainy — an impression which, however comical he may become, we are not again allowed to lose. In the first scene in which he appears, the third in the play, there is one of the most remarkable instances in dramatic literature of a man saying one thing but thinking another and the audience made to see this. He prolongs the situation, keeps the Christians on tenterhooks, turns the terms of the contract over and over in his mind, as if he were considering the soundness of it and of the borrower, while all the time he is hoping, for once in his life, that his debtor may turn out not sound but bankrupt. He casts up Antonio's hard usage of him in the past, defends the practice of interest-taking, is at the point of stipulating what the rate this time shall be, and then — decides to be friends and take no interest at all. He seems, and is, loath to part for a time with three thousand ducats — " 'tis a good round sum!" — but at the bottom of his heart he is eager.

And as for the third artifice, that a sleepy audience may not make the mistake of the cautious critic and take the villain for the hero, Shakespeare is at pains to label the villain by an aside at the moment the hero appears on the boards:

> I hate him for he is a Christian,
> But more for that in low simplicity
> He lends out money gratis, and brings down
> The rate of usance here with us in Venice.

Those are his motives, later confessed repeatedly; and either one brands him as a villain more unmistakably in that day, as we shall see, than in ours. Of the indignities which he has endured he speaks also, and of revenge; but of none of these has he anything to say at the trial. There he pleads his oath, perjury to his soul should he break it, his "lodged hate," or his "humour"; further than that, "I can give no reason nor I will not," — for some reasons a man does not give; but here to himself and later to Tubal — "were he out of Venice I can make what merchandise I will" — he tells, in the thick of the action, the unvarnished truth. As with Shakespeare's villains generally — Aaron, Iago, or Richard III — only what they say concerning their purposes aside or to their confidants can be relied upon; and Shylock's oath and his horror of perjury are, as Dr Furness observes, belied by his clutching at thrice the principal when the pound of flesh escapes him, just as is his moneylender's ruse of pretending to borrow the cash from "a friend" (avowed as such by Moses in the *School for Scandal*) by his going home "to purse the ducats straight."

His arguments, moreover, are given a specious, not to say a grotesque colouring. Similar ones used by the Jew in Silvayn's *Orator* (1596), probably known to Shakespeare, are there called "sophisticall." But Hazlitt and other critics strangely say that in argument Shylock has the best of it.

> What if my house be troubled with a rat
> And I be pleas'd to give *ten* thousand ducats
> To have it ban'd?

This particular rat is a human being; but the only thing to remark upon, in Shylock's opinion, is his willingness to squander ten thousand ducats on it instead of three. "Hates any man the thing," he cries (and there he is ticketed), "he would not kill!" Even in Hazlitt's time, moreover, a choice of "carrion flesh" in preference to ducats could not be plausibly compared as a "humour"—the Jew's gross jesting here grates upon you—with an aversion to pigs or to the sound of the bagpipe, or defended as a right by the analogy of holding slaves; nor could the practice of interest-taking find a warrant in Jacob's pastoral trickery while in the service of Laban; least of all in the day when Sir John Hawkins, who initiated the slave trade, with the Earls of Pembroke and Leicester and the Queen herself for partners, bore on the arms which were granted him for his exploits a demi-Moor, proper, in chains, and in the day when the world at large still held interest-taking to be robbery. Very evidently, moreover, Shylock is discomfited by Antonio's question, "Did he take interest?" for he falters and stumbles in his reply—

> No, not take interest, not, as you would say,
> Directly, interest,—

and is worsted, in the eyes of the audience if not in his own, by the repeated use of the old Aristotelian argument of the essential barrenness of money, still gospel in Shakespeare's day, in the second question,

> Or is your gold and silver ewes and rams?

For his answer is meant for nothing better than a piece of complacent shamelessness:

> I cannot tell: I make it breed as fast.

Only twice does Shakespeare seem to follow Shylock's pleadings and reasonings with any sympathy—"Hath a dog money?" in the first scene in which he appears, and "Hath not a Jew eyes?" in the third act—but a bit too much has been made of this. Either plea ends in such fashion as to alienate the audience. To Shylock's reproaches the admirable Antonio, "one of the gentlest and humblest of all the men in Shakespeare's theatre," praised and honoured by every one but Shylock, retorts, secure in his virtue, that he is just as like to spit on him and spurn him again. And Shylock's celebrated justification of his race runs headlong into a justification of his villainy: "The villainy which you teach me I will execute, and it shall go hard but I will better the instruction." "Hath not a Jew eyes?" and he proceeds to show that your Jew is no less than a man, and as such has a right, not to respect or compassion, as the critics for a century have had it, but to revenge. Neither large nor lofty are his claims. The speech begins with the answer to Salerio's question about the pound of flesh. "Why, I am sure, if he forfeit, thou wilt not take his flesh. What's that good for?" "To bait fish withal," he retorts in savage jest; "if it will feed nothing else it will feed my revenge;" and he goes on to complain of insults, and of thwarted bargains to the tune of half a million, and to make a plea for which he has already robbed himself of a hearing. Quite as vigorously and (in that day) with as much reason, the detestable and abominable Aaron defends his race and colour, and Edmund, the dignity of bastards. The worst of his villains Shakespeare allows to plead their cause: their confidences in soliloquy or aside, if not (as here) slight touches in the plea itself, sufficiently counteract any too favourable impression. This, on the face of it, is a plea for indulging in revenge with all its rigours; not a word is put in for the nobler side of Jewish character; and in lending Shylock his eloquence Shakespeare is but giving the devil his due.

By all the devices, then, of Shakespeare's dramaturgy Shylock is proclaimed, as by the triple repetition of a crier, to be the villain, though a comic villain or butt. Nor does the poet let pass any of the prejudices of that day which might heighten this impression. A miser, a moneylender, a Jew,—all three had from time immemorial been objects of popular detestation and ridicule, whether in life or on the stage. The union of them in one person is in Shakespeare's time the rule, both in plays and in "character"-writing: to the popular imagination a moneylender was a sordid miser with a hooked nose. So it is in the acknowledged prototype of Shylock, Marlowe's "bottle-nosed" monster, Barabas, the Jew of Malta. Though far more of a villain, he has the same traits of craft and cruelty, the same unctuous friendliness hiding a thirst for a Christian's blood, the same thirst for blood outreaching his greed for gold, and the same spirit of unrelieved egoism which thrusts aside the claims of his family, his nation, or even his faith.

If Barabas fawns like a spaniel when he pleases, grins when he bites, heaves up his shoulders when they call him dog, Shylock, for his part, "still bears it with a patient shrug," and "grows kind," seeking the Christian's "love" in the hypocritical fashion of Barabas with the suitors and the friars. If Barabas ignores the interests of his brother Jews, poisons his daughter, "counts religion but a childish toy," and, in various forms, avows the wish that "so I live perish may all the world," Shylock has no word for the generous soul but "fool" and "simpleton," and cries ("fervid patriot" that he is, "martyr and avenger"): "A diamond gone, cost me two thousand ducats in Frankfort! The curse never fell upon our nation until now. I never felt it till now." Such is his love of his race, which, Professor Raleigh says, is "deep as life." And in the next breath he cries, as "the affectionate father": "Two thousand ducats in that, and other precious, precious jewels. I would my daughter were dead at my foot, and the jewels in her ear . . . and the ducats in her coffin."

This alternation of daughter and ducats itself comes from Marlowe's play, as well as other ludicrous touches, such as your Jew's stinginess with food and horror of swine-eating, and the confounding of Jew and devil. This last is an old, widespread superstition: on the strength of holy writ the Fathers (with the suffrage in this century of Luther) held that the Jews were devils and the synagogue the house of Satan. In both plays it affords the standing joke, in the *Merchant of Venice* nine times repeated. "Let me say Amen betimes," exclaims Salerio in the midst of his good wishes for Antonio; "lest the devil cross my prayer, for here he comes in the likeness of a Jew." And in keeping with these notions Shylock's synagogue is, as Luther piously calls it, *ein Teuffels Nest*, the nest for hatching his plot once he and Tubal and the others of his "tribe" can get together. "Go, go, Tubal," he cries in the unction of his guile, "and meet me at our synagogue; go, good Tubal, at our synagogue, Tubal!" In any one such eagerness for the sanctuary is suspicious; but all the more in those times, when the congregation was of Jews and the business of a Christian's flesh. These sly and insinuating Oriental repetitions would of themselves have given the Saxon audience a shudder.

It is highly probable, moreover, that Shylock wore the red hair and beard, mentioned by Jordan, from the beginning, as well as the bottle-nose of Barabas. So Judas was made up from of old; and in their immemorial orange-tawny, high-crowned hats, and "Jewish gabardines," the very looks of the two usurers provoked derision. In both plays the word Jew, itself a badge of opprobrium, is constantly in use instead of the proper name of the character and as a byword for cruelty and cunning. . . .

Those who will have it that Shylock, though bad, was made so, do violence

to Shakespeare in two different ways. In the first place, they have recourse to
an all-pervading irony. Antonio, gentlest and humblest of Shakespeare's heroes,
kicking and spitting at Jews and thrusting salvation down their throats, — such,
they say, is the spectacle of race-hatred pointed at by the poet. And those others
who will have it that Shylock is a noble spirit brought to shame, carry the irony
still further, into the characterization of Antonio and his friends. He, not Shylock,
is the caricature: his virtues are but affectations and shams; his friends are parasites,
spendthrifts, and fribbles! They make no effort to raise the three thousand ducats
to save him, they do not even provide him with a surgeon against his need.
That is, nothing is what it seems; a comedy ending in moonlight blandishments
and badinage is a tragedy, and the play written for the customers of the Globe
flies over their honest heads to the peaks of nineteenth-century criticism. Irony
is surely unthinkable unless the author intends it, and here not the slightest trace
of such an intention appears. Moreover, a play of Shakespeare's is self-contained;
the irony is within it, so to speak, not underneath it. There is irony in the
appearance of Banquo at the moment when Macbeth presumes hypocritically
to wish for his presence at the feast; or, more obviously still, in the fulfilment
of the Witches' riddling oracles; but there is no irony, as we have seen, such
as Mr Yeats discovers in the success of Henry V and the failure of Richard II.
There is irony in the situation of a king so powerful reduced to a state so pitiful,
before he has "shook off the regal thoughts wherewith he reigned"; but Shakespeare
does not dream that to fail and be a Richard is better than to succeed and be
a Henry — or an Antonio. He knows not the way of thinking which lightly sets
the judgment of the world aside, nor the ways of modern artistic expression,
which almost withholds the purport of the higher judgment from the world.
No abysmal irony undermines his solid sense and straightforward meaning. Shylock
is indeed condemned; Sir Henry Irving took no counsel of the poet when he
made his exit from the ducal palace in pathetic triumph.

Nor is Jessica treated with malice, in mockery or irony, as, having forsaken
him and robbed him and never since given him a regretful or pitying thought,
she now revels in jest and sentiment, in moonlight and melody, at Belmont.
What right has Signor Croce to call her ecstasy sensual? Since her father had
made home a hell to her and Launcelot, and in robbing him she has acted with
the approval of everybody, as did the son who robbed Harpagon, has she not
a right, in the world where she now lives, to be really happy? Signor Croce
may be horrified at Jessica as was Rousseau at the unfilial Cléante; but just as
sympathy at the theatre traditionally is for the debtor and against the moneylender, so it is for the amorous son or eloping daughter and against the hard-
hearted, stingy father. Thus it had been on the stage since the days of Plautus;
cheating the old man was both sport for the slave and relief for the son's necessities.
Either consideration gave pleasure in the comic theatre. It is not ideal justice—

that is not the business of comedy; but as Monsieur Donnay says of Harpagon's gold, "nous sommes enchantés que cet or, mal acquis, rentre dans la circulation. De tous les vices qui peuvent s'emparer d'un homme, l'avarice est certainement le plus détestable, et qui excite le moins notre pitié."

And as for the Jew — " 'tis charity to undo a Jew," both thought and said the age. Indeed, is not Jessica what might have been taken for a true daughter of her tribe, like Rachel, who "stole the images that were her father's" before she fled; and like the daughters of Israel, who before they went up out of the land of Egypt, "borrowed" of their neighbours jewels of silver and jewels of gold? "And they spoiled the Egyptians," adds naïvely and complacently the ancient chronicler; and, having turned Christian, why should not Jessica spoil the Jew? the Christians will be likely to ask. But here, as in Antonio's notion of conversion, or the Duke's notion of clemency to Jews, is the irony of history, not of art. Shakespeare's thought is as simple and sincere as is the old hagiographer's about the balancing of Jews' ledgers by royal edict — pacem operatur justicia.

In the second place, they do violence to Shakespeare, as Mr Hudson observes, in representing Shylock as the product of his environment. The thoughts of men had hardly begun to run in such channels; the ancient rigours of retribution held fast; men still believed in heaven and hell, in villains and heroes. Though in Shakespeare there is little of George Eliot's moral austerity, as brought to bear on Tito Melema, for instance, Mr Yeats errs, I think, in the opinion that his plays are, like all great literature, "written in the spirit of the Forgiveness of Sin." Macbeth is not forgiven, nor is Othello. Richard III and Iago were damned even in the making. Though the shortcomings of Falstaff, Bardolph, Pistol, and Nym serve a while as food for mirth, Shakespeare is in full accord with Henry V as he casts his fellows out of his company and out of his mind, to meet their end, maybe, in the brothel or on the gallows. And he is in full accord with Portia and the Duke in the judgment scene. Except in comedy, he has not the spirit of forgiveness which, like Uncle Toby's towards the Devil, comes of mere kindness of heart; and neither in comedy nor in tragedy has he the forgiveness of our psychological and social drama and novel, where both villains and heroes are no more, which comes of fulness of knowledge. Thus he deals with poverty, the hard-hearted, greasy, foul-smelling, ignorant, and ungrateful multitude, for which he so often utters his aversion; and thus he deals with the kindred subject of heredity. If a scoundrel is a bastard, or is mean of birth, the fact is not viewed as an extenuating circumstance, but is turned to a reproach. It may in a sense explain his depravity, but never explain it away. It sets the seal upon it. It confirms the prejudice that there is a difference between noble blood and that of low degree. So, though our hearts are softened by Shylock's recital of the indignities he has suffered, the hearts of the Elizabethans, by a simpler way of thinking, are hardened.

It confirms the prejudice that there is a difference betwixt Christian and Jew. The Fathers, Protestant theologians like Luther, seventeenth-century lawyers like Coke and Prynne, review the pitiful story of the Jews in Europe grimly, with at best a momentary and furtive pathos. It proves their notion of the curse. What else, in an age when it was the universal belief that Jew and Gentile alike took upon their heads the curse of Adam's sin on issuing from the mother's womb? Even today a man who is abused in the street is supposed, by bystanders, to deserve it: the world barks at rags and poverty like the dogs: and everyone knows that there are certain scars (as of branding) and certain diseases (though people without them may be equally guilty) which a canny man does not complain of or betray. And how much more in the days of literary and theological bludgeoning; when the reformers were to the common enemy, and to one another, dogs, hogs, and asses; when Shakespeare himself let one of his noblest characters cast it up to another that he possessed but one trunk of clothes; when Milton was reviled, in scholarly Latin, for his blindness and (in defiance of fact) for his guttering eyelids; and when Dryden never heard the last of the beating he got at the instigation of a fellow poet in a London street. For everything there is some one to blame, is the point of view, and who so much as he who has the worst of it?

> And every loss the men of Jebus bore,
> They still were thought God's enemies the more!

Such is the logic of Luther as he puts to the Jews the crushing question (naïvely exhorting Christians, if they must speak to Jews at all, to do likewise, and "not to quarrel with them"): "Hear'st thou, Jew, dost thou know that Jerusalem, your temple, and your priesthood have been destroyed now over fourteen hundred and sixty years?" Even at the end of the seventeenth century Robert South, as he considers the universal detestation in which, through the ages, Jews have been held, must conclude that there is "some peculiar vileness essentially fixed in the genius of this people." That no one is to blame does not occur to him, or that the cause of the detestation lies in race-hatred, the incompatibility of temperament and customs. "What's his reason?" cries Shylock. It is the reason which Antonio—that is Shakespeare—is not analytical enough to recognize or cynical enough to avow. Steadily the Jewishness of Shylock is kept before us; like Barabas, he loses his name in his nationality—"the Jew," "the dog Jew," "the villain Jew," "his Jewish heart";—and it is not merely according to the measure of his villainy that at the end and throughout the play he suffers. With Robert South Shakespeare himself might have said that the reason was his "essential Jewish *vileness*"; but we, who, in the light of modern psychology and the history of society, are aware that no man and no age can render adequately the reason why they themselves do anything, recognize that the famous reason given by Shylock himself, in the heat of his *ex parte* pleading with which Shakespeare so little sympathizes, curiously enough hits the mark. . . .

Then there is inversion, the tables turned. "L'histoire du persécuteur victime de sa persécution, du dupeur dupé, du voleur volé, fait le fond de bien des comédies." The trial scene is an example. To most critics Shylock has here seemed to be more or less pathetic, despite the fact that, as I take it, Shakespeare has employed almost every possible means to produce a contrary, quite incompatible effect.

Professor Baker holds that Shakespeare evinces a sense of dramatic values in presenting Shylock's disappointment as tragic in his own eyes, amusing in Gratiano's. How is the tragic value presented? By the miser and usurer's prostrate prayer to the Duke to take his life if he would take his wealth, or by the plea that he is not well? The biter bitten, is the gibe cast at him at the end of *Il Pecorone*; and that, exactly, is the spirit of the scene. It is the same spirit and almost the same situation as at the close of Sheridan's *Duenna*, where another Jew, not nearly so culpable as Shylock, having now been fast married to the dragon herself, not, as he thinks, to the maiden that she guards, is jeered at for it, while one of the characters gives the reason, — that "there is not a fairer subject for contempt and ridicule than a knave become the dupe of his own art." Shylock's disappointment is tragic to him, but good care is taken that it shall not be to us. Shakespeare is less intent on values than on the conduct and direction of our sympathies through the scene. This he manages both by the action and the comment. The scene is a rise and a fall, a triumph turned into a defeat, an apparent tragedy into a comedy; and the defeat is made to repeat the stages of the triumph so as to bring home to us the fact — the comic fact — of retribution. When fortune turns, almost all the steps of the ladder whereby Shylock with scales and knife had climbed to clutch the fruit of revenge he must now descend empty-handed and in bitterness; and what had been offered to him and refused by him, he is now, when he demands it again, refused. With the course of the action the comment is in perfect accord and unison, marking and signalizing the stages of Shylock's fall. The outcries against the Jew and his stony heart, of the Duke, Bassanio, and Gratiano — protested against by Antonio as futile — give place to the jeers of Gratiano and the irony of the fair judge. Gratiano is not the only one to crow. "Thou shalt have justice, more than thou desir'st — Soft! The Jew shall have all justice — Why doth the Jew pause? Take thy forfeiture — Tarry, Jew; the law hath yet another hold on you — Art thou contented, Jew? What dost thou say?" Aimed at Shylock as he pleads and squirms, these words fall from lips which had a moment before extolled the heavenly qualities of mercy! But for more than the meagre mercy which Shylock is shown there is neither time nor place, the crowing fits the latter part of the action as perfectly as the indignant comment had fitted the earlier, and we must equally accept it or divest the scene of meaning and sense. The Jew's very words are echoed by Portia and Gratiano as they jeer, and at every turn that the course of justice takes (welcomed by Shylock, while it was in his favour, with hoarse cries of gloating and triumph) there are now peals and shouts of laughter, such laughter as arises when Tartuffe the hypocrite is caught by Orgon, — "un rire se lève de tous les coins de la salle, un rire de vengeance si vous voulez, un rire amer, un rire violent." The running fire assails him to the very moment — and beyond it — that Shylock says he is not well, and staggers out, amid Gratiano's jeers touching his baptism, to provoke in the audience the laughter of triumph and vengeance in his own day and bring tears to their eyes in ours. How can we here for a moment sympathize with Shylock unless at the same time we indignantly turn, not only against Gratiano, but against Portia, the Duke, and all Venice as well? But Shakespeare's scene it is — Shakespeare's comedy, — not ours or Hazlitt's.

One reason why the critics have, despite all, even in this scene, found pathos in Shylock, is that they well know that comic effects may keep company with the pathetic, in Shakespeare as in Dostoevsky and Chekhov. They remember Mercutio's last words, Mrs Quickly's report of Falstaff's death, or the Fool's babblings in *King Lear*. Laughter may indeed blend with tears when the character is treated tenderly; but here and in the daughter-ducats scene it is, as I have said, only the laughter of derision. In the judgment scene, moreover, there is — very clearly marked — the spirit of retaliation; it is a harsh and vindictive laughter; and if Shakespeare had here intended any minor and momentary pathetic effects such as critics nowadays discover, he simply overwhelms them. Professor Matthews says that Shakespeare meant the spectators to hate Shylock and also to laugh at him, and yet made him pathetic — supremely pathetic too. The combination seems to me impossible, at least in a comedy, and Professor Matthews seems to me to be talking metaphysics and forgetting the stage which he knows so well. If hateful, Shylock would provoke in the audience the *rire de vengeance*, an echo of Gratiano's jeer; if pathetic also, he would — and should — provoke no laughter (at least of such kind as is known to me) at all. In comedy, at any rate, things must be simple and clear-cut; a character which is to provoke laughter cannot be kept, like Buridan's ass, in equilibrium, exciting, at the same time, both sympathy and hatred. For then the audience will keep its equilibrium too.

Portia's Failure

Harold C. Goddard

When Shylock enters the courtroom he is in a more rational if not less determined state than when we last saw him. He is no longer unwilling to listen, and the moderate, almost kindly words of the Duke,

> We all expect a gentle answer, Jew,

lead us to hope that even at the eleventh hour he may relent.

Shylock's answer to the Duke is one of the most remarkable evidences of Shakespeare's overt interest in psychological problems in any of the earlier plays. The passage is sufficient in itself to refute the idea that it is "modernizing" to detect such an interest on his part. Naturally Shylock does not talk about complexes, compulsions, and unconscious urges, but he recognizes the irrational fear of pigs and cats in the concrete for what it is, a symbol of something deeper that is disturbing the victim. He senses in himself the working of similar forces too tremendous for definition, too powerful to oppose even though he feels them driving him—*against his will and to his shame*, he implies—to commit the very offense that has been committed against him. Imagine Richard III or Iago speaking in that vein! If this be "villainy," it is of another species. Here is the main theme of the play in its profoundest implication. For what is the relation of what is conscious to what is unconscious if not the relation of what is on the surface to what is underneath? Thus Shylock himself—and through him Shakespeare—hands us the key: to open the casket of this play we must look beneath *its* surface, must probe the unconscious minds of its characters.

From *The Meaning of Shakespeare.* © 1951 by The University of Chicago. The University of Chicago Press, 1951. Originally entitled "*The Merchant of Venice.*"

You'll ask me why I rather choose to have
A weight of carrion flesh than to receive
Three thousand ducats. I'll not answer that;
But say it is my humour. Is it answer'd?
What if my house be troubled with a rat
And I be pleas'd to give ten thousand ducats
To have it ban'd? What, are you answer'd yet?
Some men there are love not a gaping pig;
Some, that are mad if they behold a cat;
And others, when the bagpipe sings i' the nose,
Cannot contain their urine: for affection,
Mistress of passion, sways it to the mood
Of what it likes or loathes. Now, for your answer:
As there is no firm reason to be render'd
Why he cannot abide a gaping pig;
Why he, a harmless necessary cat;
Why he, a wauling bagpipe; but of force
Must yield to such inevitable shame
As to offend, himself being offended;
So can I give no reason, nor I will not,
More than a lodg'd hate and a certain loathing
I bear Antonio, that I follow thus
A losing suit against him. Are you answer'd?

(Note, especially, that "losing suit"!)

Antonio recognizes the futility of opposing Shylock's passion with reason. You might as well argue with a wolf, he says, tell the tide not to come in, or command the pines not to sway in the wind. The metaphors reveal his intuition that what he is dealing with is not ordinary human feeling within Shylock but elemental forces from without that have swept in and taken possession of him. And Gratiano suggests that the soul of a wolf has infused itself with the Jew's. Shylock's hatred does have a primitive quality. But Gratiano did not need to go back to the wolves, or even to Pythagoras, to account for it. It is elemental in character because it comes out of something vaster than the individual wrongs Shylock has suffered: the injustice suffered by his ancestors over the generations. As Hazlitt finely remarks: "He seems the depositary of the vengeance of his race." It is this that gives him that touch of sublimity that all his fierceness cannot efface. The bloody Margaret of *Henry VI*, when she becomes the suffering Margaret of *Richard III*, is endowed with something of the same tragic quality. If this man is to be moved, it must be by forces as far above reason as those that now animate him are below it.

And then Portia enters.

The introduction and identifications over, Portia, as the Young Doctor of Laws, says to Shylock:

> Of a strange nature is the suit you follow;
> Yet in such rule that the Venetian law
> Cannot impugn you as you do proceed.

This bears the mark of preparation, if not of rehearsal. It seems a strange way of beginning, like a partial prejudgment of the case in Shylock's favor. But his hopes must be raised at the outset to make his ultimate downfall the more dramatic. "Do you confess the bond?" she asks Antonio. "I do," he replies.

> Then must the Jew be merciful.

Portia, as she says this, is apparently still addressing Antonio. It would have been more courteous if, instead of speaking of him in the third person, she had turned directly to Shylock and said, "Then must you be merciful." But she makes a worse slip than that: the word *must*. Instantly Shylock seizes on it, pouring all his sarcasm into the offending verb:

> On what compulsion "*must*" I? Tell me that.

Portia is caught! You can fairly see her wheel about to face not so much the Jew as the unanswerable question the Jew has asked. He is right—she sees it: "must" and "mercy" have nothing to do with each other; no law, moral or judicial, can force a man to be merciful.

For a second, the question must have thrown Portia off balance. This was not an anticipated moment in the role of the Young Doctor. But forgetting the part she is playing, she rises to the occasion superbly. The truth from Shylock elicits the truth from her. Instead of trying to brush the Jew aside or hide behind some casuistry or technicality, she frankly sustains his exception:

> The quality of mercy is not strain'd.

"I was wrong, Shylock," she confesses in effect. "You are right"; mercy is a matter of grace, not of constraint:

> It droppeth as the gentle rain from heaven
> Upon the place beneath.

Shylock, then, supplied not only the cue, but, we might almost say, the first line of Portia's most memorable utterance.

In all Shakespeare—unless it be Hamlet with "To be or not to be"—there is scarcely another character more identified in the world's mind with a single speech than Portia with her words on mercy. And the world is right. They have a "quality" different from anything else in her role. They are no prepared words of the Young Doctor she is impersonating, but her own, as unexpected as was Shylock's disconcerting question. Something deep down in him draws them from something deep down—or shall we say high up?—in her. They are the spiritual gold hidden not beneath lead but beneath the "gold" of her superficial life, her reward for meeting Shylock's objection with sincerity rather than with evasion.

A hush falls over the courtroom as she speaks them (as it does over the audience when *The Merchant of Venice* is performed). Even the Jew is moved. Who can doubt it? Who can doubt that for a moment at least he is drawn back from the brink of madness and logic on which he stands? Here is the celestial visitant—the Portia God made—sent expressly to exorcise the demonic powers that possess him. Only an insensible clod could fail to feel its presence. And Shylock is no insensible clod. Can even he show mercy? Will a miracle happen? It is the supreme moment. The actor who misses it misses everything.

And then, incredibly, it is Portia who fails Shylock, not Shylock Portia. The same thing happens to her that happened to him at that other supreme moment when he offered Antonio the loan without interest. Her antipodal self emerges. In the twinkling of an eye, the angel reverts to the Doctor of Laws. "So quick bright things come to confusion." Whether the actress in Portia is intoxicated by the sound of her own voice and the effect it is producing, or whether she feels the great triumph she has rehearsed being stolen from her if Shylock relents, or both, at any rate, pushing aside the divine Portia and her divine opportunity, the Young Doctor resumes his role. His "therefore, Jew" gives an inkling of what is coming. You can hear, even in the printed text, the change of voice, as Portia sinks from compassion to legality:

> I have spoke thus much
> To mitigate the justice of thy plea,
> Which if thou follow, this strict court of Venice
> Must needs give sentence 'gainst the merchant there.

It would be unbelievable if the words were not there. "You should show mercy," the Young Doctor says in effect, "but if you don't, this court will be compelled to decide in your favor." It is as if a mother, having entreated her son to desist from some wrong line of conduct and feeling she had almost won, were to conclude: "I hope you won't do it, but, if you insist, I shall have to let you, since your father told you you could." It is like a postscript that undoes the letter. Thus Portia the lover of mercy is deposed by Portia the actress that the latter may have the rest of her play. And the hesitating Shylock, pushed back to the precipice, naturally has nothing to say but

> My deeds upon my head! I crave the law,
> The penalty and forfeit of my bond.

The rest of the scene is an overwhelming confirmation of Portia's willingness to sacrifice the human to the theatrical, a somewhat different kind of sacrifice from that referred to in the inscription on the leaden casket. If there was any temptation that Shakespeare understood, it must have been this one. I was his own temptation. And, as he tells us in the *Sonnets*, he nearly succumbed to it:

> And almost thence my nature is subdu'd
> To what it works in, like the dyer's hand.

Portia's *was* subdued.

The skill with which from this point she stages and acts her play proves her a consummate playwright, director, and actress — three in one. She wrings the last drop of possible suspense from every step in the mounting excitement. She stretches every nerve to the breaking point, arranges every contrast, climax, and reversal with the nicest sense for maximum effect, doing nothing too soon or too late, holding back her "Tarry a little" until Shylock is on the very verge of triumph, even whetting his knife perhaps. It is she who says to Antonio, "Therefore lay bare your bosom." It is she who asks if there is a balance ready to weigh the flesh, a surgeon to stay the blood. And she actually allows Antonio to undergo his last agony, to utter, uninterrupted, his final farewell.

It is at this point that the shallow Bassanio reveals an unsuspected depth in his nature by declaring, with a ring of sincerity we cannot doubt, that he would sacrifice everything, including his life and his wife, to save his friend.

> *Who chooseth me must give and hazard all he hath.*

It is now, not when he stood before it, that Bassanio proves worthy of the leaden casket. Called on to make good his word, he doubtless would not have had the strength. But that does not prove that he does not mean what he says at the moment. And at that moment all Portia can do to help him is to turn into a jest — which she and Nerissa are alone in a position to understand — the most heartfelt and noble words her lover ever uttered.

> POR.: Your wife would give you little thanks for that,
> If she were by to hear you make the offer.

This light answer, in the presence of what to Antonio and Bassanio is the very shadow of death, measures her insensibility to anything but the play she is presenting, the role she is enacting.

From this jest, in answer to the Jew's insistence, she turns without a word of transition to grant Shylock his sentence:

> A pound of that same merchant's flesh is thine.
> The court awards it, and the law doth give it . . .
> And you must cut this flesh from off his breast.
> The law allows it, and the court awards it.

It is apparently all over with Antonio. The Jew lifts his knife. But once more appearances are deceitful. With a "tarry a little" this mistress of the psychological moment plays in succession, one, two, three, the cards she has been keeping back for precisely this moment. Now the Jew is caught in his own trap, now he gets a taste of his own logic, a dose of his own medicine. Now there is no more talk of mercy, but justice pure and simple, an eye for an eye:

> POR.: as thou urgest justice, be assur'd
> Thou shalt have justice, more than thou desir'st.

Seeing his prey about to elude him, Shylock is now willing to accept the offer of three times the amount of his bond, and Bassanio actually produces the money. He is willing to settle on those terms. But not Portia:

> The Jew shall have all justice; soft! no haste:
> He shall have nothing but the penalty.

Shylock reduces his demand: he will be satisfied with just his principal. Again Bassanio has the money ready. But Portia is adamant:

> He shall have merely justice, and his bond.

When the Jew pleads again for his bare principal, she repeats:

> Thou shalt have nothing but the forfeiture,

and as he moves to leave the courtroom, she halts him with a

> Tarry, Jew:
> The law hath yet another hold on you.

All this repetition seems enough to make the point clear. But that the "beauty" of the nemesis may be lost on no one in the courtroom (nor on the dullest auditor when *The Merchant of Venice* is performed) Shakespeare has the gibing Gratiano on the spot to rub in the justice of the retribution: "O learned judge!" "O upright judge!" "A second Daniel, a Daniel, Jew!" "A second Daniel!" over and over. Emily Dickinson has spoken of "the mob within the heart." Gratiano is the voice of that mob, and he sees to it that a thrill of vicarious revenge runs down the spine of every person in the theater. So exultant are we at seeing the biter bit.

Why are we blind to the ignominy of identifying ourselves with the most brutal and vulgar character in the play? Obviously because there is a cruel streak in all of us that is willing to purchase excitement at any price. And excitement exorcises judgment. Only when we are free of the gregarious influences that dominate us in an audience does the question occur: What possessed Portia to torture not only Antonio but her own husband with such superfluous suspense? She knew what was coming. Why didn't she let it come at once? Why didn't she invoke immediately the law prescribing a penalty for any alien plotting against the life of any citizen of Venice instead of waiting until she had put those she supposedly loved upon the rack? The only possible answer is that she wanted a spectacle, a dramatic triumph with herself at the center. The psychology is identical with that which led the boy Kolya in *The Brothers Karamazov* to torture his sick little friend Ilusha by holding back the news that his lost dog was found, merely in order to enjoy the triumph of restoring him to his chum at the last moment in the presence of an audience. In that case the result was fatal. The child died from the excitement.

To all this it is easy to imagine what those will say who hold that Shakespeare was first the playwright and only incidentally poet and psychologist. "Why, but this is just a play!" they will exclaim, half-amused, half-contemptuous, "and a comedy at that! Portia! It isn't Portia who contrives the postponement. It is Shakespeare. Where would his play have been if his heroine had cut things short or failed to act exactly as she did?" Where indeed? Which is precisely why the poet made her the sort of woman who would have acted under the given conditions exactly as she did act. That was his business: not to find or devise situations exciting in the theater (any third-rate playwright can do that) but to discover what sort of men and women would behave in the often extraordinary ways in which they are represented as behaving in such situations in the stories he inherited and selected for dramatization.

"Logic is like the sword," says Samuel Butler, "—those who appeal to it shall perish by it." Never was the truth of that maxim more clearly illustrated than by Shylock's fate. His insistence that his bond be taken literally is countered by Portia's insistence that it be taken even more literally—and Shylock "perishes."

He who had been so bent on defending the majesty of the law now finds himself in its clutches, half his goods forfeit to Antonio, the other half to the state, and his life itself in peril.

And so Portia is given a second chance. She is to be tested again. She has had her legal and judicial triumph. Now it is over will she show to her victim that quality which at her own divine moment she told us "is an attribute to God himself"? The Jew is about to get his deserts. Will Portia forget her doctrine that mercy is mercy precisely because it is not deserved? The Jew is about to receive justice. Will she remember that our prayers for mercy should teach us to do the deeds of mercy and that in the course of justice none of us will see salvation? Alas! she will forget, she will not remember. Like Shylock, but in a subtler sense, she who has appealed to logic "perishes" by it.

Up to this point she has been forward enough in arrogating to herself the function of judge. But now, instead of showing compassion herself or entreating the Duke to, she motions Shylock to his knees:

> Down therefore and beg mercy of the Duke.

"Mercy"! This beggar's mercy, though it goes under the same name, has not the remotest resemblance to that quality that drops like the gentle rain from heaven. Ironically it is the Duke who proves truer to the true Portia than Portia herself.

> DUKE: That thou shalt see the difference of our spirits,
> I pardon thee thy life before thou ask it.

And he suggests that the forfeit of half of Shylock's property to the state may be commuted to a fine.

> Ay, for the state; not for Antonio,

Portia quickly interposes, as if afraid that the Duke is going to be too merciful, going to let her victim off too leniently. Here, as always, the aftermath of too much "theatrical" emotion is a coldness of heart that is like lead. The tone in which Portia has objected is reflected in the hopelessness of Shylock's next words:

> Nay, take my life and all! Pardon not that!
> You take my house when you do take the prop
> That doth sustain my house. You take my life
> When you do take the means whereby I live.

Portia next asks Antonio what "mercy" he can render. And even the man whom Shylock would have killed seems more disposed than Portia to mitigate the severity of his penalty: he is willing to forgo the half of Shylock's goods if the Duke will permit him the use of the other half for life with the stipulation that it go to Lorenzo (and so to Jessica) at his death. But with two provisos: that all the Jew dies possessed of also go to Lorenzo-Jessica and that

He presently become a Christian.

Doubtless the Elizabethan crowd, like the crowd in every generation since including our own, thought that this was letting Shylock off easily, that this *was* showing mercy to him. Crowds do not know that mercy is wholehearted and has nothing to do with halves or other fractions. Nor do crowds know that you cannot make a Christian by court decree. Antonio's last demand quite undoes any tinge of mercy in his earlier concessions.

Even Shylock, as we have seen, had in him at least a grain of spiritual gold, of genuine Christian spirit. Only a bit of it perhaps. Seeds do not need to be big. Suppose that Portia and Antonio, following the lead of the seemingly willing Duke, had watered this tiny seed with that quality that blesses him who gives as well as him who takes, had overwhelmed Shylock with the grace of forgiveness! What then? The miracle, it is true, might not have taken place. Yet it might have. But instead, as if in imitation of the Jew's own cruelty, they whet their knives of law and logic, of reason and justice, and proceed to cut out their victim's heart. (That that is what it amounts to is proved by the heartbroken words,

I pray you give me leave to go from hence.
I am not well.)

Shylock's conviction that Christianity and revenge are synonyms is confirmed. "If a Christian wrong a Jew, what should his sufferance be by Christian example? Why, revenge." The unforgettable speech from which that comes, together with Portia's on mercy, and Lorenzo's on the harmony of heaven, make up the spiritual argument of the play. Shylock asserts that a Jew is a man. Portia declares that man's duty to man is mercy — which comes from heaven. Lorenzo points to heaven but laments that the materialism of life insulates man from its harmonies. A celestial syllogism that puts to shame the logic of the courtroom.

That Shakespeare planned his play from the outset to enforce the irony of Portia's failure to be true to her inner self in the trial scene is susceptible of something as near proof as such things can ever be. As in the case of Hamlet's

A little more than kin, and less than kind,

the poet, over and over, makes the introduction of a leading character seemingly casual, actually significant. Portia enters *The Merchant of Venice* with the remark that she is aweary of the world. Nerissa replies with that wise little speech about the illness of those that surfeit with too much (an observation that takes on deeper meaning in the retrospect after we realize that at the core what is the trouble with Portia and her society is boredom). "Good sentences and well pronounced," says Portia, revealing in those last two words more than she knows. "They would be better if well followed," Nerissa pertinently retorts. Whereupon Portia, as if gifted with insight into her own future, takes up Nerissa's theme:

> If to do were as easy as to know what were good to do, chapels had been churches, and poor men's cottages princes' palaces. It is a good divine that follows his own instructions: I can easier teach twenty what were good to be done, than be one of the twenty to follow mine own teaching.

If that is not a specific preparation for the speech on mercy and what follows it, what in the name of coincidence is it? The words on mercy were good sentences, well pronounced. And far more than that. But for Portia they remained just words in the sense that they did not teach her to do the deeds of mercy. So, a few seconds after we see her for the first time, does Shakespeare let her pass judgment in advance on the most critical act of her life. For a moment, at the crisis in the courtroom, she seems about to become the leaden casket with the spiritual gold within. But the temptation to gain what many men desire — admiration and praise — is too strong for her and she reverts to her worldly self. Portia is the golden casket.

Wealth's Communion and an Intruder

C. L. Barber

> Should I go to church
> And see the holy edifice of stone
> And not bethink me straight of dangerous rocks,
> Which, touching but my gentle vessel's side,
> Would scatter all her spices on the stream,
> Enrobe the roaring waters with my silks,
> And, in a word, but even now worth this,
> And now worth nothing?

When Nashe, in *Summer's Last Will and Testament*, brings on a Christmas who is a miser and refuses to keep the feast, the killjoy figure serves, as we have noticed, to consolidate feeling in support of holiday. Shakespeare's miser in *The Merchant of Venice* has the same sort of effect in consolidating the gay Christians behind Portia's "The quality of mercy is not strained." The comic antagonist as we get him in Nashe's churlish Christmas, uncomplicated by such a local habitation as Shakespeare developed for Shylock, is a transposed image of the pageant's positive spokesmen for holiday. Summer reminds him, when he first comes on, of the role he ought to play, and his miserliness is set off against the generosity proper to festivity:

> SUMMER. Christmas, how chance thou com'st not as the rest,
> Accompanied with some music, or some song?
> A merry carol would have grac'd thee well;
> Thy ancestors have us'd it heretofore.
>
> CHRISTMAS. Aye, antiquity was the mother of ignorance: this latter

From *Shakespeare's Festive Comedy*. © 1959 by Princeton University Press. Originally entitled "The Merchants and the Jew of Venice: Wealth's Communion and an Intruder."

world, that sees but with her spectacles, hath spied a pad in
those sports more than they could.

SUMMER. What, is't against thy conscience for to sing?

CHRISTMAS. No, nor to say, by my troth, if I may get a good bargain.

SUMMER. Why, thou should'st spend, thou should'st not to care to
get. Christmas is god of hospitality.

CHRISTMAS. So will he never be of good husbandry. I may say to
you, there is many an old god that is now grown out of fashion.
So is the god of hospitality.

SUMMER. What reason canst thou give he should be left?

CHRISTMAS. No other reason, but that Gluttony is a sin, and too
many dunghills are infectious. A man's belly was not made for
a powdering beef tub: to feed the poor twelve days, and let
them starve all the year after, would but stretch out the guts
wider than they should be, and so make famine a bigger den
in their bellies than he had before. . . .

AUTUMN. [Commenting on Christmas]
A fool conceits no further than he sees,
He hath no sense of aught but what he feels.

CHRISTMAS. Aye, aye, such wise men as you come to beg at such
fool's doors as we be.

AUTUMN. Thou shut'st thy door; how should we beg of thee? . . .

CHRISTMAS. *Liberalitas liberalitate perit*; . . . our doors must have
bars, our doublets must have buttons. . . . Not a porter that
brings a man a letter, but will have his penny. I am afraid to
keep past one or two servants, lest, hungry knaves, they should
rob me: and those I keep, I warrant I do not pamper up too
lusty; I keep them under with red herring and poor John all
the year long. I have damned up all my chimnies.

Here is the stock business about denying food and locking up which appears
also in Shylock's part, along with a suggestion of the harsh ironical humor that
bases itself on "the facts" — "aye, such wise men as you come to beg at such
fool's doors as we be" — and also a moment like several in *The Merchant of Venice*
where the fangs of avarice glint naked — "if I may get a good bargain." Shylock,
moreover, has the same attitude as Nashe's miser about festivity:

What, are there masques? Hear you me, Jessica.
Lock up my doors; and when you hear the drum
And the vile squealing of the wry-neck'd fife,
Clamber not you up to the casements then,

> Nor thrust your head into the public street
> To gaze on Christian fools with varnish'd faces;
> But stop my house's ears—I mean my casements.
> Let not the sound of shallow fopp'ry enter
> My sober house.
>
> (II.v.28–36)

Lorenzo's enterprise in stealing Jessica wins our sympathy partly because it is done in a masque, as a merriment:

> BASSANIO. . . . put on
> Your boldest suit of mirth, for we have friends
> That purpose merriment...
>
> (II.ii.210–12)

> LORENZO. Nay, we will slink away at supper time,
> Disguise us at my lodging, and return
> All in an hour.
> GRATIANO. We have not made good preparation.
> SALERIO. We have not spoke us yet of torchbearers.
> SOLANIO. 'Tis vile, unless it may be quaintly ordered.
>
> (II.iv.1–6)

The gallants are sophisticated, like Mercutio, about masquerade; but this masque *is* "quaintly ordered," because, as Lorenzo confides to Gratiano,

> Fair Jessica shall be my torchbearer.
>
> (II.iv.40)

The episode is another place where Shakespeare has it come true that nature can have its way when people are in festive disguise. Shylock's "tight" opposition, "fast bind, fast find" (II.v.54) helps to put us on the side of the "masquing mates," even though what they do, soberly considered, is a gentlemanly version of raiding the Lombard quarter or sacking bawdy houses on Shrove Tuesday.

MAKING DISTINCTIONS ABOUT THE USE OF RICHES

The Merchant of Venice as a whole is not shaped by festivity in the relatively direct way that we have traced in *Love's Labour's Lost* and *A Midsummer Night's Dream*. The whirling away of daughter and ducats is just one episode in a complex plot which is based on story materials and worked out with much more concern for events, for what happens next, than there is in the two previous comedies. This play was probably written in 1596, at any rate fairly early in the first period of easy mastery which extends from *Romeo and Juliet, A Midsummer Night's Dream,* and *Richard II* through the Henry IV and V plays and *As You Like It* to *Julius Caesar* and *Twelfth Night.* At the opening of this period, the two comedies modeled directly on festivities represent a new departure, from which Shakespeare returns in *The Merchant of Venice* to write a comedy with a festive emphasis, but one which is rather more "a kind of history" and less "a gambold." The play's large structure is developed from traditions which are properly theatrical; it is not a theatrical adaptation of a social ritual. And yet analogies to social occasions and rituals prove to be useful in understanding the symbolic action. I shall be pursuing such analogies without suggesting, in most cases, that there is a direct influence from the social to the theatrical form. Shakespeare here is working with autonomous mastery, developing a style of comedy that makes a festive form for feeling and awareness out of all the theatrical elements, scene, speech, story, gesture, role which his astonishing art brought into organic combination.

Invocation and abuse, poetry and railing, romance and ridicule — we have seen repeatedly how such complementary gestures go to the festive celebration of life's powers, along with the complementary roles of revellers and killjoys, wits and butts, insiders and intruders. What is mocked, what kind of intruder disturbs the revel and is baffled, depends on what particular sort of beneficence is being celebrated. *The Merchant of Venice,* as its title indicates, exhibits the beneficence of civilized wealth, the something-for-nothing which wealth gives to those who use it graciously to live together in a humanly knit group. It also deals, in the role of Shylock, with anxieties about money, and its power to set men at odds. Our econometric age makes us think of wealth chiefly as a practical matter, an abstract concern of work, not a tangible joy for festivity. But for the new commercial civilizations of the Renaissance, wealth glowed in luminous metal, shone in silks, perfumed the air in spices. Robert Wilson, already in the late eighties, wrote a pageant play in the manner of the moralities, *Three Lords and Three Ladies of London,* in which instead of Virtues, London's Pomp and London's Wealth walked gorgeously and smugly about the stage. Despite the terrible sufferings some sections of society were experiencing, the 1590's were a period when London was becoming conscious of itself as wealthy and cultivated, so that it could consider great commercial Venice as a prototype. And yet there were at the same time traditional suspicions of the profit motive and newly urgent anxieties about the power of money to disrupt human relations. Robert Wilson also wrote, early in the eighties, a play called *The Three Ladies of London,* where instead of London's Wealth and Pomp we have Lady Lucar and the attitude towards her which her name implies. It was in expressing and so coping with these anxieties about money that Shakespeare developed in Shylock a comic antagonist far more important than any such figure had been in his earlier comedies. His play is still centered in the celebrants rather than the intruder, but Shylock's part is so fascinating that already in 1598 the comedy was entered in the stationer's register as "a book of the Merchant of Venice, or otherwise called the Jew of Venice." Shylock's name has become a byword because of the superb way that he embodies the evil side of the power of money, its ridiculous and pernicious consequences in anxiety and destructiveness. In creating him and setting him over against Antonio, Bassanio, Portia, and the rest, Shakespeare was making distinctions about the use of riches, not statically, of course, but dynamically, as distinctions are made when a social group sorts people out, or when an organized social ritual does so. Shylock is the opposite of what the Venetians are; but at the same time he is an embodied irony, troublingly like them. So his role is like that of the scapegoat in many of the primitive rituals which Frazer has made familiar, a figure in whom the evils potential in a social organization are embodied, recognized and enjoyed during a period of licence, and then in due course abused, ridiculed, and expelled.

The large role of the antagonist in *The Merchant of Venice* complicates the movement through release to clarification: instead of the single outgoing of *A Midsummer Night's Dream*, there are two phases. Initially there is a rapid, festive movement by which gay youth gets something for nothing, Lorenzo going masquing to win a Jessica gilded with ducats, and Bassanio sailing off like Jason to win the golden fleece in Belmont. But all this is done against a background of anxiety. We soon forget all about Egeus' threat in *A Midsummer Night's Dream*, but we are kept aware of Shylock's malice by a series of interposed scenes. Will Summer said wryly about the Harvest merrymakers in *Summer's Last Will and Testament*, "As lusty as they are, they run on the score with George's wife for their posset." We are made conscious that running on the score with Shylock is a very dangerous business, and no sooner is the joyous triumph accomplished at Belmont than Shylock's malice is set loose. It is only after the threat he poses has been met that the redemption of the prodigal can be completed by a return to Belmont.

The key question in evaluating the play is how this threat is met, whether the baffling of Shylock is meaningful or simply melodramatic. Certainly the plot, considered in outline, seems merely a prodigal's dream coming true: to have a rich friend who will set you up with one more loan so that you can marry a woman both beautiful and rich, girlishly yielding and masterful; and on top of that to get rid of the obligation of the loan because the old moneybags from whom your friend got the money is proved to be so villainous that he does not deserve to be paid back! If one adds humanitarian and democratic indignation at anti-Semitism, it is hard to see, from a distance, what there can be to say for the play: Shylock seems to be made a scapegoat in the crudest, most dishonest way. One can apologize for the plot, as Middleton Murry and Granville-Barker do, by observing that it is based on a fairy-story sort of tale, and that Shakespeare's method was not to change implausible story material, but to invent characters and motives which would make it acceptable and credible, moment by moment, on the stage. But it is inadequate to praise the play for delightful and poetic incoherence. Nor does it seem adequate to say, as E. E. Stoll does, that things just do go this way in comedy, where old rich men are always baffled by young and handsome lovers, lenders by borrowers. Stoll is certainly right, but the question is whether Shakespeare has done something more than merely appeal to the feelings any crowd has in a theater in favor of prodigal young lovers and against old misers. As I see it, he has expressed important things about the relations of love and hate to wealth. When he kept to old tales, he not only made plausible protagonists for them, but also, at any rate when his luck held, he brought up into a social focus deep symbolic meanings. Shylock is an ogre, as Middleton Murry said, but he is the ogre of money power. The old tale of the pound of flesh involved taking literally the proverbial metaphors about moneylenders "taking it out of the hide" of their victims, eating them up. Shakespeare keeps the unrealistic literal business, knife-sharpening and all; we accept it, because he makes it express real human attitudes:

> If I can catch him once upon the hip,
> I will feed fat the ancient grudge I bear him.
> (I.iii.47–48)

So too with the fairy-story caskets at Belmont: Shakespeare makes Bassanio's prodigal fortune meaningful as an expression of the triumph of human, social relations over the relations kept track of by accounting. The whole play dramatizes the conflict between the mechanisms of wealth and the masterful, social use of it. The happy ending, which abstractly considered as an event is hard to credit, and the treatment of Shylock, which abstractly considered as justice is hard to justify, *work* as we actually watch or read the play because these events express relief and triumph in the achievement of a distinction.

To see how this distinction is developed, we need to attend to the tangibles of imaginative design which are neglected in talking about plot. So, in the two first scenes, it is the seemingly incidental, random talk that establishes the gracious, opulent world of the Venetian gentlemen and of the "lady richly left" at Belmont, and so motivates Bassanio's later success. Wealth in this world is something profoundly social, and it is relished without a trace of shame when Salerio and Salanio open the play by telling Antonio how rich he is:

> Your mind is tossing on the ocean;
> There where your argosies with portly sail—

> Like signiors and rich burghers on the flood,
> Or, as it were, the pageants of the sea —
> Do overpeer the petty traffickers,
> That cursy to them, do them reverence,
> As they fly by them with their woven wings.
> (I.i.8–14)

Professor Venezky points out that Elizabethan auditors would have thought not only of the famous Venetian water ceremonies but also of "colorfully decorated pageant barges" on the Thames or of "pageant devices of huge ships which were drawn about in street shows." What is crucial is the ceremonial, social feeling for wealth. Salerio and Salanio do Antonio reverence just as the petty traffickers of the harbor salute his ships, giving way to leave him "with better company" when Bassanio and Gratiano arrive. He stands at ease, courteous, relaxed, melancholy (but not about his fortunes, which are too large for worry), while around him moves a shifting but close-knit group who "converse and waste the time together" (III.iv.12), make merry, speak "an infinite deal of nothing" (I.i.114), propose good times: "Good signiors, both, when shall we laugh? say, when?" (I.i.66). When Bassanio is finally alone with the royal merchant, he opens his mind with

> To you, Antonio,
> I owe the most, in money and in love.
> (I.i.130–31)

Mark Van Doren, in his excellent chapter on this play, notes how these lines summarize the gentleman's world where "there is no incompatibility between money and love." So too, one can add, in this community there is no conflict between enjoying Portia's beauty and her wealth: "her sunny locks/Hang on her temples like a golden fleece." When, a moment later, we see Portia mocking her suitors, the world suggested is, again, one where standards are urbanely and humanly social: the sad disposition of the county Palatine is rebuked because (unlike Antonio's) it is "unmannerly." Yet already in the first scene, though Shylock is not in question yet, the anxiety that dogs wealth is suggested. In the lines which I have taken as an epigraph for this chapter, Salerio's mind moves from attending church — from safety, comfort, and solidarity — through the playful association of the "holy edifice of stone" with "dangerous rocks," to the thought that the sociable luxuries of wealth are vulnerable to impersonal forces:

> rocks,
> Which, touching but my gentle vessel's side,

> Would scatter all her spices on the stream,
> Enrobe the roaring waters with my silks...
>
> (I.i.31–34)

The destruction of what is cherished, of the civic and personal, by ruthless impersonal forces is sensuously immediate in the wild waste of shining silk on turbulent water, one of the magic, summary lines of the play. Earlier there is a tender, solicitous suggestion that the vessel is the more vulnerable because it is "gentle"—as later Antonio is gentle and vulnerable when his ships encounter "the dreadful touch/Of merchant-marring rocks" (III.ii.270–71) and his side is menaced by a "stony adversary" (IV.i.4).

When Shylock comes on in the third scene, the easy, confident flow of colorful talk and people is checked by a solitary figure and an unyielding speech:

SHYLOCK. Three thousand ducats—well.
BASSANIO. Ay, sir, for three months.
SHYLOCK. For three months—well.
BASSANIO. For the which, as I told you, Antonio shall be bound.
SHYLOCK. Antonio shall become bound—well.
BASSANIO. May you stead me? Will you pleasure me? Shall I know
    your answer?
SHYLOCK. Three thousand ducats for three months, and Antonio
    bound.

(I.iii.1–10)

We can construe Shylock's hesitation as playing for time while he forms his plan. But more fundamentally, his deliberation expresses the impersonal logic, the mechanism, involved in the control of money. Those *well's* are wonderful in the way they bring bland Bassanio up short. Bassanio assumes that social gestures can brush aside such consideration:

SHYLOCK. Antonio is a good man.
BASSANIO. Have you heard any imputation to the contrary?
SHYLOCK. Ho, no, no, no, no! My meaning in saying he is a good
    man, is to have you understand me that he is sufficient.

(I.iii.12–17)

The laugh is on Bassanio as Shylock drives his hard financial meaning of "good man" right through the center of Bassanio's softer social meaning. The Jew goes on to calculate and count. He connects the hard facts of money with the rocky sea hazards of which we have so far been only picturesquely aware: "ships are but boards"; and he betrays his own unwillingness to take the risks proper to commerce: "and other ventures he hath, squand'red abroad."

> I think I may take his bond.
> BASSANIO. Be assur'd you may.
> SHYLOCK. I will be assur'd I may; and, that I may be assured,
> I will bethink me.
>
> (I.iii.28–31)

The Jew in this encounter expresses just the things about money which are likely to be forgotten by those who have it, or presume they have it, as part of a social station. He stands for what we mean when we say that "money is money." So Shylock makes an ironic comment — and *is* a comment, by virtue of his whole tone and bearing — on the folly in Bassanio which leads him to confuse those two meanings of "good man," to ask Shylock to dine, to use in this business context such social phrases as "Will you *pleasure* me?" When Antonio joins them, Shylock (after a soliloquy in which his plain hatred has glittered) becomes a pretender to fellowship, with an equivocating mask:

> SHYLOCK. This is kind I offer.
> BASSANIO. This were kindness.
> SHYLOCK. This kindness will I show.
>
> (I.iii.143–44)

We are of course in no doubt as to how to take the word "kindness" when Shylock proposes "in a merry sport" that the penalty be a pound of Antonio's flesh.

In the next two acts, Shylock and the accounting mechanism which he embodies are crudely baffled in Venice and rhapsodically transcended in Belmont. The solidarity of the Venetians includes the clown, in whose part Shakespeare can use conventional blacks and whites about Jews and misers without asking us to take them too seriously:

> To be ruled by my conscience, I should stay with the Jew my master,
> who (God bless the mark) is a kind devil. . . . My master's a very Jew.
>
> (I.iii.24–25, 104–5)

Even the street urchins can mock Shylock after the passion which "the dog Jew did utter in the streets":

> Why, all the boys in Venice follow him,
> Crying his stones, his daughter, and his ducats.
>
> (II.viii.23–24)

TRANSCENDING RECKONING AT BELMONT

The simplest way to describe what happens at Belmont is to say that Bassanio is lucky; but Shakespeare gives a great deal of meaning to his being lucky. His choosing of the casket might be merely theatrical; but the play's handling of the age-old story motif makes it an integral part of the expression of relations between people and possessions. Most of the argument about gold, silver, and lead is certainly factitious, even tedious. It must necessarily be so, because the essence of a lottery is a discontinuity, something hidden so that the chooser cannot get from here to there by reasoning. Nerissa makes explicit a primitive notion of divination:

> Your father was ever virtuous; and holy men at their death have good
> inspirations. Therefore the lott'ry that he hath devised in these three
> chests of gold, silver, and lead, whereof who chooses his meaning
> chooses you, will no doubt never be chosen by any rightly but one
> who shall rightly love.
>
> (I.ii.30–36)

The elegant phrasing does not ask us to take the proposition very seriously, but Nerissa is pointing in the direction of a mystery. Part of the meaning is that love is not altogether a matter of the will, however willing. Portia recognizes this even when her heart is in her mouth as Bassanio is about to choose:

> Away then! I am lock'd in one of them.
> If you do love me, you will find me out.
> Nerissa and the rest, stand all aloof.
> Let music sound while he doth make his choice...
>
> (III.ii.40–43)

The song, "Tell me, where is fancy bred," serves to emphasize the break, the speechless pause while Bassanio chooses. The notion that it serves as a signal to warn Bassanio off gold and silver is one of those busybody emendations which eliminate the dramatic in seeking to elaborate it. The dramatic point is precisely that there is no signal: "Who chooseth me must give and hazard all he hath" (II.vii.16).

If we look across for a moment at Shylock, thinking through opposites as the play's structure invites us to do, his discussion with Antonio about the "thrift" of Jacob and the taking of interest proves to be relevant to the luck of the caskets. Antonio appeals to the principle that interest is wrong because it involves no risk:

> This was a venture, sir, that Jacob serv'd for;
> A thing not in his power to bring to pass,
> But sway'd and fashion'd by the hand of heaven.
>
> (I.iii.92–94)

One way to get a fortune is to be fortunate: the two words fall together significantly at the conclusion of the opening scene:

> BASSANIO. O my Antonio, had I but the means
>   To hold a rival place with one of them,
>   I have a mind presages me such thrift
>   That I should questionless be fortunate!
> ANTONIO. Thou know'st that all my fortunes are at sea...
>   (I.i.173–77)

Antonio's loan is venture capital. It fits with this conception that Bassanio, when at Belmont he goes "to my fortune and the caskets," turns away from money, from "gaudy gold,/Hard food for Midas," and from silver, the "pale and common drudge/'Tween man and man" (III.ii.101–04). Money is not used to get money; that is the usurer's way:

> ANTONIO. Or is your gold and silver ewes and rams?
> SHYLOCK. I cannot tell; I make it breed as fast.
>   (I.iii.96–97)

Instead Bassanio's borrowed purse is invested in life—including such lively things as the "rare new liveries" (II.ii.117) that excite Launcelot, and the "gifts of rich value" which excite Nerissa to say

> A day in April never came so sweet
> To show how costly summer was at hand
> At this fore-spurrer comes before his lord.
>   (II.ix.93–95)

With the money, Bassanio invests *himself*, and so risks losing himself—as has to be the case with love. (Antonio's commitment of his body for his friend is in the background.) It is a limitation of the scene where he makes his choice that the risk has to be conveyed largely by the poetry, since the outward circumstances are not hazardous. Portia describes Bassanio as

> young Alcides when he did redeem
> The virgin tribute paid by howling Troy
> To the sea monster. . . . Go, Hercules!
> Live thou, I live.

>   (III.ii.55–61)

Of course we know that these are lover's feelings. But the moment of choice is expressed in terms that point beyond feelings to emphasize discontinuity; they convey the experience of being lost and giddily finding oneself again in a new situation. The dramatic shift is all the more vividly rendered in the language since gesture here can do little. Portia speaks of an overwhelming ecstasy of love when "all the other passions fleet to air" (III.ii.108). Bassanio likens himself to an athlete

> Hearing applause and universal shout,
> Giddy in spirit, still gazing in a doubt
> Whether those peals of praise be his or no.
>
> (III.ii.143–45)

He describes in a wonderful way the experience of being disrupted by joy:

> Madam, you have bereft me of all words,
> Only my blood speaks to you in my veins;
> And there is such confusion in my powers
> As, after some oration fairly spoke
> By a beloved prince, there doth appear
> Among the buzzing pleased multitude,
> Where every something, being blent together,
> Turns to a wild of nothing, save of joy,
> Express'd and not express'd.
>
> (III.ii.175–83)

This poetry is remarkable for the conscious way that it describes being carried beyond expression, using words to tell of being beyond them. The lines in which Portia gives herself and her possessions to Bassanio make explicit, by an elaborate metaphor of accounting, that what is happening sets the accounting principle aside:

> You see me, Lord Bassanio, where I stand,
> Such as I am. Though for myself alone
> I would not be ambitious in my wish
> To wish myself much better, yet for you
> I would be trebled twenty times myself,
> A thousand times more fair, ten thousand times more rich,
> That, only to stand high in your account,
> I might in virtues, beauties, livings, friends,
> Exceed account. But the full sum of me
> Is sum of nothing, which, to term in gross,
> Is an unlesson'd girl, unschool'd, unpractic'd.
>
> (III.ii.149–59)

This is extravagant, and extravagantly modest, as fits the moment; but what is telling is the way the lines move from possessions, through the paradox about sums, to the person in the midst of them all, "where I stand," who cannot be added up. It is she that Bassanio has won, and with her a way of living for which his humanity, breeding, and manhood can provide a center:

> Happiest of all is that her gentle spirit
> Commits itself to yours to be directed,
> As from her lord, her governor, her king.
>   (III.ii.163–65)

The possessions *follow* from this human, social relation.

COMICAL/MENACING MECHANISM IN SHYLOCK

But the accounting mechanism which has been left behind by Bassanio and Portia has gone on working, back at Venice, to put Antonio at Shylock's mercy, and the anxiety it causes has to be mastered before the marriage can be consummated,

> For never shall you lie by Portia's side
> With an unquiet soul.
>   (III.ii.305–06)

Historical changes in stock attitudes have made difficulties about Shylock's role as a butt, not so much in the theater, where it works perfectly if producers only let it, but in criticism, where winds of doctrine blow sentiments and abstractions about. The Elizabethans almost never saw Jews except on the stage, where Marlowe's Barabas was familiar. They did see *one*, on the scaffold, when Elizabeth's unfortunate physician suffered for trumped-up charges of a poisoning plot. The popular attitude was that to take interest for money was to be a loan shark — though limited interest was in fact allowed by law. An aristocrat who like Lord Bassanio ran out of money commanded sympathy no longer felt in a middle-class world. Most important of all, suffering was not an absolute evil in an era when men sometimes embraced it deliberately, accepted it as inevitable, and could watch it with equanimity. Humanitarianism has made it necessary for us to be much more thoroughly insulated from the human reality of people if we are to laugh at their discomfiture or relish their suffering. During the romantic period, and sometimes more recently, the play was presented as a tragi-comedy, and actors vied with one another in making Shylock a figure of pathos. I remember a very moving scene, a stock feature of romantic productions, in which George Arliss came home after Bassanio's party, lonely and tired and old, to knock in vain at the door of the house left empty by Jessica. How completely unhistorical the romantic treatment was, E. E. Stoll demonstrated overwhelmingly in his essay on Shylock in 1911, both by wide-ranging comparisons of Shylock's role with others in Renaissance drama and by analysis of the *optique du théâtre*.

To insert a humanitarian scene about Shylock's pathetic homecoming prevents the development of the scornful amusement with which Shakespeare's text presents the miser's reaction in Solanio's narrative:

> I never heard a passion so confus'd,
> So strange, outrageous, and so variable,
> As the dog Jew did utter in the streets.
> "My daughter! O my ducats! O my daughter!
> Fled with a Christian! O my Christian ducats!"
>
> (II.viii.12–16)

Marlowe had done such a moment already with Barabas hugging in turn his moneybags and his daughter — whom later the Jew of Malta poisons with a pot of porridge, as the Jew of Venice later wishes that Jessica "were hears'd at my foot, and the ducats in her coffin" (III.i.93–94). But the humanitarian way of playing the part develops suggestions that are *also* in Shakespeare's text:

> I am bid forth to supper, Jessica.
> There are my keys. But wherefore should I go?
> I am not bid for love; they flatter me.
> But yet I'll go in hate, to feed upon
> The prodigal Christian.
>
> (II.v.11–15)

Shakespeare's marvelous creative sympathy takes the stock role of Jewish usurer and villain and conveys how it would feel to be a man living inside it. But this does not mean that he shrinks from confronting the evil and the absurdity that go with the role; for the Elizabethan age, to understand did not necessarily mean to forgive. Shylock can be a thorough villain and yet be allowed to express what sort of treatment has made him what he is:

> You call me misbeliever, cutthroat dog,
> And spet upon my Jewish gaberdine,
> And all for use of that which is mine own.
>
> (I.iii.112–14)

We can understand his degradation and even blame the Antonios of Venice for it; yet it remains degradation:

> Thou call'dst me dog before thou hadst a cause;
> But, since I am a dog, beware my fangs.
>
> (III.iii.6–7)

Shylock repeatedly states, as he does here, that he is only finishing what the Venetians started. He can be a drastic ironist, because he carries to extremes what is present, whether acknowledged or not, in their silken world. He insists that money is money—and they cannot do without money either. So too with the rights of property. The power to give freely, which absolute property confers and Antonio and Portia so splendidly exhibit, is also a power to refuse, as Shylock so logically refuses:

> You have among you many a puchas'd slave,
> Which, like your asses and your dogs and mules,
> You use in abject and in slavish parts,
> Because you bought them. Shall I say to you,
> "Let them be free, marry them to you heirs!"
>
> You will answer,
> "The slaves are ours." So do I answer you.
> The pound of flesh which I demand of him
> Is dearly bought, 'tis mine, and I will have it.
> (IV.i.90–100)

At this point in the trial scene, Shylock seems a juggernaut that nothing can stop, armed as he is against a pillar of society by the principles of society itself: "If you deny me, fie upon your law! . . . I stand for judgement. Answer. Shall I have it." Nobody does answer him here, directly; instead there is an interruption for Portia's entrance. To answer him is the function of the whole dramatic action, which is making a distinction that could not be made in direct, logical argument.

Let us follow this dramatic action from its comic side. Shylock is comic, so far as he is so, because he exhibits what should be human, degraded into mechanism. The reduction of life to mechanism goes with the miser's wary calculation, with the locking up, with the preoccupation with "that which is mine own." Antonio tells Bassanio that

> My purse, my person, my extremest means
> Lie all unlock'd to your occasions.
> (I.i.138–39)

How open! Antonio has to live inside some sort of rich man's melancholy, but at least he communicates with the world through outgoing Bassanio (and, one can add, through the commerce which takes his fortunes out to sea). Shylock, by contrast, who breeds barren metal, wants to keep "the vile squeeling of the wryneck'd fife" out of his house, and speaks later, in a curiously revealing, seemingly random illustration, of men who "when the bagpipe sings i'th'nose,/

Cannot contain their urine" (V.i.49–50). Not only is he closed up tight inside himself, but after the first two scenes, we are scarcely allowed by his lines to feel with him. And we never encounter him alone; he regularly comes on to join a group whose talk has established an outside point of view towards him. This perspective on him does not exclude a potential pathos. There is always potential pathos, behind, when drama makes fun of isolating, anti-social qualities. Indeed, the process of *making fun of* a person often works by exhibiting pretensions to humanity so as to show that they are inhuman, mechanical, not validly appropriate for sympathy. With a comic villain such as Shylock, the effect is mixed in various degrees between our responding to the mechanism as menacing and laughing at it as ridiculous.

So in the great scene in which Solanio and Salerio taunt Shylock, the potentiality of pathos produces effects which vary between comedy and menace:

> SHYLOCK. You knew, none so well, none so well as you, of my
> daughter's flight.
> SALERIO. That's certain. I, for my part, knew the tailor that made
> the wings she flew withal.
>
> (III.i.27–30)

Shylock's characteristic repetitions, and the way he has of moving ahead through similar, short phrases, as though even with language he was going to use only what was his own, can give an effect of concentration and power, or again, an impression of a comically limited, isolated figure. In the great speech of self-justification to which he is goaded by the two bland little gentlemen, the iteration conveys the energy of anguish:

> — and what's his reason? I am a Jew. Hath not a Jew eyes? Hath
> not a Jew hands, organs, dimensions, senses, affections, passions?
> fed with the same food, hurt with the same weapons, subject to the
> same diseases, healed by the same means, warmed and cooled by the
> same winter and summer as a Christian is? If you prick us, do we
> not bleed? If you tickle us, do we not laugh? If you poison us, do
> we not die? And if you wrong us, shall we not revenge? If we are
> like you in the rest, we will resemble you in that.
>
> (III.i.60–71)

Certainly no actor would deliver this speech without an effort at pathos; but it is a pathos which, as the speech moves, converts to menace. And the pathos is qualified, limited, in a way which is badly falsified by humanitarian renderings that open all the stops at "Hath not a Jew hands, etc. . . ." For Shylock thinks to claim only a *part* of humanness, the lower part, physical and passional. The similar self-pitying enumeration which Richard II makes differs significantly in going from "live with bread like you" to social responses and needs, "Taste grief,/Need friends" (*R.II*, III.ii.175–176). The passions in Shylock's speech are conceived as reflexes; the parallel clauses draw them all towards the level of "tickle . . . laugh." The same assumption, that the passions and social responses are mechanisms on a par with a nervous tic, appears in the court scene when Shylock defends his right to follow his "humor" in taking Antonio's flesh:

> As there is no firm reason to be rend'red
> Why he cannot abide a gaping pig,
> Why he a harmless necessary cat,
> Why he a woollen bagpipe—but of force
> Must yield to such inevitable shame
> As to offend himself, being offended;
> So can I give no reason, nor I will not,
> More than a lodg'd hate and a certain loathing
> I bear unto Antonio...
>
> (IV.i.52–61)

The most succinct expression of this assumption about man is Shylock's response to Bassanio's incredulous question:

> BASSANIO. Do all men kill the things they do not love?
> SHYLOCK. Hates any man the thing he would not kill?
>
> (IV.i.66–67)

There is no room in this view for mercy to come in between "wrong us" and "shall we not revenge?" As Shylock insists, there is Christian example for him: the irony is strong. But the mechanism of stimulus and response is only a part of the truth. The reductive tendency of Shylock's metaphors, savagely humorous in Iago's fashion, goes with this speaking only the lower part of the truth. He is not cynical in Iago's aggressive way, because as an alien he simply doesn't participate in many of the social ideals which Iago is concerned to discredit in self-justification. But the two villains have the same frightening, ironical power from moral simplification.

Shylock becomes a clear-cut butt at the moments when he is himself caught in compulsive, reflexive responses, when instead of controlling mechanism he is controlled by it: "O my daughter! O my ducats!" At the end of the scene of taunting, his menace and his pathos become ridiculous when he dances like a jumping jack in alternate joy and sorrow as Tubal pulls the strings:

> TUBAL. Yes, other men have ill luck too. Antonio, as I heard
> in Genoa—

SHYLOCK. What, what, what? Ill luck, ill luck?

TUBAL. Hath an argosy cast away coming from Tripolis.

SHYLOCK. I thank God, I thank God! — Is it true? is it true?

TUBAL. I spoke with some of the sailors that escaped the wrack.

SHYLOCK. I thank thee, good Tubal. Good news, good news!
Ha, ha! Where? in Genoa?

TUBAL. Your daughter spent in Genoa, as I heard, one night fourscore ducats.

SHYLOCK. Thou stick'st a dagger in me. I shall never see my gold
again. Fourscore ducats at a sitting! Fourscore ducats!

TUBAL. There came divers of Antonio's creditors in my company to
Venice that swear he cannot choose but break.

SHYLOCK. I am very glad of it. I'll plague him; I'll torture him.
I am glad of it.

TUBAL. One of them show'd me a ring that he had of your daughter
for a monkey.

SHYLOCK. Out upon her! Thou torturest me, Tubal. It was my
turquoise; I had it of Leah when I was a bachelor. I would not
have given it for a wilderness of monkeys.

TUBAL. But Antonio is certainly undone.

SHYLOCK. Nay, that's true, that's very true.

(III.i.102–30)

This is a scene in the dry manner of Marlowe, Jonson, or Molière, a type of comedy not very common in Shakespeare: its abrupt alternations in response convey the effect Bergson describes so well in *Le Rire*, where the comic butt is a puppet in whom motives have become mechanisms that usurp life's self-determining pre-rogative. Some critics have left the rhythm of the scene behind to dwell on the pathos of the ring he had from Leah when he was a bachelor. It is like Shakespeare once to show Shylock putting a gentle sentimental value on something, to match the savage sentimental value he puts on revenge. There *is* pathos; but it is being fed into the comic mill and makes the laughter all the more hilarious.

THE COMMUNITY SETTING ASIDE ITS MACHINERY

In the trial scene, the turning point is appropriately the moment when Shylock gets caught in the mechanism he relies on so ruthlessly. He narrows everything down to his roll of parchment and his knife: "Till thou canst rail the seal from off my bond . . ." (IV.i.139). But two can play at this game:

> as thou urgest justice, be assur'd
> Thou shalt have justice more than thou desir'st.

(IV.i.315–16)

Shylock's bafflement is comic, as well as dramatic, in the degree that we now see through the threat that he has presented, recognizing it to have been, in a degree, unreal. For it is unreal to depend so heavily on legal form, on fixed verbal definition, on the mere machinery by which human relations are controlled. Once Portia's legalism has broken through his legalism, he can only go on the way he started, weakly asking "Is that the law?" while Gratiano's jeers underscore the comic symmetry:

> A Daniel still say I, a second Daniel!
> I thank thee, Jew, for teaching me that word.
> (IV.i.340–41)

The turning of the tables is not, of course, simply comic, except for the bold, wild and "skipping spirit" of Gratiano. The trial scene is a species of drama that uses comic movement in slow motion, with an investment of feeling such that the resolution is in elation and relief colored by amusement, rather than in the evacuation of laughter. Malvolio, a less threatening killjoy intruder, is simply laughed out of court, but Shylock must be ruled out, with jeering only on the side lines. The threat Shylock offers is, after all, drastic, for legal instruments, contract, property are fundamental. Comic dramatists often choose to set them hilariously at naught; but Shakespeare is, as usual, scrupulously responsible to the principles of social order (however factitious his "law" may be literally). So he produced a scene which exhibits the limitations of legalism. It works by a dialectic that carries to a more general level what might be comic reduction to absurdity. To be tolerant, because we are all fools; to forgive, because we are all guilty—the two gestures of the spirit are allied, as Erasmus noted in praising the sublime folly of following Christ. Shylock says before the trial "I'll not be made a soft and dull-ey'd fool" by "Christian intercessors" (III.iii.14–15). Now when he is asked how he can hope for mercy if he renders none, he answers: "What judgement shall I dread, doing no wrong?" As the man who will not acknowledge his own share of folly ends by being more foolish than anyone else, so Shylock, who will not acknowledge a share of guilt, ends by being more guilty—and more foolish, to judge by results. An argument between Old Testament legalism and New Testament reliance on grace develops as the scene goes forward. (Shylock's references to Daniel in this scene, and his constant use of Old Testament names and allusions, contribute to the contrast.) Portia does not deny the bond—nor the law behind it; instead she makes such a plea as St. Paul made to his compatriots:

> Therefore, Jew,
> Though justice be thy plea, consider this—
> That, in the course of justice, none of us

> Should see salvation. We do pray for mercy,
> And that same prayer doth teach us all to render
> The deeds of mercy.
>
> (IV.i.97–102)

Mercy becomes the word that gathers up everything we have seen the Venetians enjoying in their reliance on community. What is on one side an issue of principles is on the other a matter of social solidarity: Shylock is not one of the "we" Portia refers to, the Christians who say in the Lord's Prayer "Forgive us our debts as we forgive our debtors." All through the play the word Christian has been repeated, primarily in statements that enforce the fact that the Jew is outside the easy bonds of community. Portia's plea for mercy is a sublime version of what in less intense circumstances, among friends of a single communion, can be conveyed with a shrug or a wink:

> Dost thou hear, Hal? Thou knowest in the state of innocency Adam
> fell; and what should poor Jack Falstaff do in the days of villany?
>
> (*I H. IV*, III.iii.185–88)

Falstaff, asking for an amnesty to get started again, relies on his festive solidarity with Hal. Comedy, in one way or another, is always asking for amnesty, after showing the moral machinery of life getting in the way of life. The machinery as such need not be dismissed—Portia is very emphatic about not doing that. But social solidarity, resting on the buoyant force of a collective life that transcends particular mistakes, can set the machinery aside. Shylock, closed off as he is, clutching his bond and his knife, cannot trust this force, and so acts only on compulsion:

> PORTIA.   Do you confess the bond?
> ANTONIO. I do.
> PORTIA.   Then must the Jew be merciful.
> SHYLOCK. On what compulsion must I? Tell me that.
> PORTIA. The quality of mercy is not strain'd;
>   It droppeth as the gentle rain from heaven
>   Upon the place beneath. It is twice blest—
>   It blesseth him that gives, and him that takes.
>
> (IV.i.181–87)

It has been in giving and taking, beyond the compulsion of accounts, that Portia, Bassanio, Antonio have enjoyed the something-for-nothing that Portia here summarizes in speaking of the gentle rain from heaven.

SHARING IN THE GRACE OF LIFE

The troth-plight rings which Bassanio and Gratiano have given away are all that remain of plot to keep the play moving after the trial. It is a slight business, but it gives the women a teasing way to relish the fact that they have played the parts of men as they give up the liberty of that disguise to become wives. And the play's general subject is continued, for in getting over the difficulty, the group provides one final demonstration that human relationships are stronger than their outward signs. Once more, Bassanio expresses a harassed perplexity about obligations in conflict; and Portia gayly pretends to be almost a Shylock about this lover's bond, carrying the logic of the machinery to absurd lengths before showing, by the new gift of the ring, love's power to set debts aside and begin over again.

No other comedy, until the late romances, ends with so full an expression of harmony as that which we get in the opening of the final scene of *The Merchant of Venice*. And no other final scene is so completely without irony about the joys it celebrates. The ironies have been dealt with beforehand in baffling Shylock; in the moment of relief after expelling an antagonist, we do not need to look at the limitations of what we have been defending. So in *Summer's Last Will and Testament*, when Summer is confronted by a miserly Christmas, he comes out wholeheartedly for festivity, whereas elsewhere, confronting spokesmen for festivity, he is always wry about it. He dismisses Christmas with

> Christmas, I tell thee plain, thou art a snudge,
> And wer't not that we love thy father well,
> Thou shouldst have felt what 'longs to Avarice.
> It is the honor of nobility
> To keep high days and solemn festivals —
> Then to set their magnificence to view,
> To frolic open with their favorites,
> And use their neighbors with all courtesy,
> When thou in hugger-mugger spend'st thy wealth.
> Amend thy manners, breathe thy rusty gold:
> Bounty will win thee love, when thou art old.

The court compels Shylock to breathe his gold and give bounty to Lorenzo. He is plainly told that he is a snudge — and we are off to noble magnificence and frolic at Belmont. No high day is involved, though Shakespeare might easily have staged the solemn festival due after Portia's wedding. Instead Lorenzo and Jessica feel the harmony of the universe and its hospitality to life in a quiet moment of idle talk and casual enjoyment of music. There is an opening out to experience in their exquisite outdoor poetry which corresponds to the openness stressed by Nashe in contrast to miserly hugger-mugger.

> The moon shines bright. In such a night as this,
> When the sweet wind did gently kiss the trees
> And they did make no noise—in such a night
> Troilus methinks mounted the Troyan walls
> And sigh'd his soul towards the Grecian tents,
> Where Cressid lay that night.
>
> (V.i.1–6)

The openness to experience, the images of reaching out towards it, or of welcoming it, letting music "creep in our ears," go with the perception of a gracious universe such as Portia's mercy speech invoked:

> How sweet the moonlight sleeps upon this bank!
> Here will we sit and let the sounds of music
> Creep in our ears. Soft stillness and the night
> Become the touches of sweet harmony.
> Sit, Jessica. Look how the floor of heaven
> Is thick inlaid with patens of bright gold.
> There's not the smallest orb which thou behold'st
> But in his motion like an angel sings...
>
> (V.i.54–61)

Lorenzo is showing Jessica the graciousness of the Christian world into which he has brought her; and it is as richly golden as it is musical! Jessica is already at ease in it, to the point of being able to recall the pains of famous lovers with equanimity, rally her lover on his vows and turn the whole thing off with "I would out-night you did no body come,/But hark, I hear the footing of a man." That everybody is so perfectly easy is part of the openness:

> LORENZO. Who comes so fast in silence of the night.
> MESSENGER. A friend.
> LORENZO. A friend? What friend? Your name, I
>   pray you, friend?...
>
> Sweet soul, let's in, and there expect their coming.
> And yet no matter. Why should we go in?
> ... bring your music forth into the air.
>
> (V.i.25–27, 51–54)

As the actual music plays, there is talk about its Orphic power, and we look back a moment toward Shylock

> The man that hath no music in himself
> Nor is not mov'd with concord of sweet sounds,
> Is fit for treasons, stratagems, and spoils...
>
> (V.i.82–84)

A certain contemplative distance is maintained by talking *about* perception, *about* harmony and its conditions, even while enjoying it. Portia comes on exclaiming how far the candle throws its beams, how much sweeter the music sounds than by day. There are conditions, times, and seasons, to be observed; but the cosmological music, which cannot be heard directly at all, is behind the buoyant decorum of the people:

> How many things by season season'd are
> To their right praise and true perfection!
> Peace ho! The moon sleeps with Endymion
> And would not be awak'd.
>
> (V.i.107–10)

At the end of the play, there is Portia's news of Antonio's three argosies richly come to harbor, and the special deed of gift for Lorenzo—"manna in the way/Of starved people." Such particular happy events are—not sentimental because Shakespeare has floated them on an expression of a tendency in society and nature which supports life and expels what would destroy it.

I must add, after all this praise for the way the play makes its distinction about the use of wealth, that *on reflection*, not when viewing or reading the play, but when thinking about it, I find the distinction, as others have, somewhat too easy. While I read or watch, all is well, for the attitudes of Shylock are appallingly inhuman, and Shakespeare makes me feel constantly how the Shylock attitude rests on a lack of faith in community and grace. But when one thinks about the Portia-Bassanio group, not in opposition to Shylock but alone (as Shakespeare does not show them), one can be troubled by their being so very very far above money:

> What, no more?
> Pay him six thousand, and deface the bond.
> Double six thousand and then treble that...
>
> (III.ii.298–300)

It would be interesting to see Portia say no, for once, instead of always yes: after all, Nashe's miser has a point, *"Liberalitas liberalitate perit."* One can feel a difficulty too with Antonio's bland rhetorical question:

> when did friendship take
> A breed of barren metal of his friend?
>
> (I.iii.134–35)

Elizabethan attitudes about the taking of interest were unrealistic: while Sir Thomas Gresham built up Elizabeth's credit in the money market of Antwerp, and the government regulated interest rates, popular sentiment continued on the level of thinking Antonio's remark reflects. Shakespeare's ideal figures and sentiments are open here to ironies which he does not explore. The clown's role just touches them when he pretends to grumble

> We were Christians enow before, e'en as many as could well live
> by one another. This making of Christians will raise the price of hogs.
>
> (III.v.23–26)

In a later chapter we shall see, in *As You Like It*, a more complete confronting of ironies, which leaves, I feel, a cleaner aftertaste. Shakespeare could no doubt have gone beyond the naïve economic morality of Elizabethan popular culture, had he had an artistic need. But he did not, because in the antithetical sort of comic form he was using in this play, the ironical function was fulfilled by the heavy contrasts embodied in Shylock.

About Shylock, too, there is a difficulty which grows on reflection, a difficulty which may be felt too in reading or performance. His part fits perfectly into the design of the play, and yet he is so alive that he raises an interest beyond its design. I do not think his humanity spoils the design, as Walter Raleigh and others argued, and as was almost inevitable for audiences who assumed that to be human was to be ipso-facto good. But it is true that in the small compass of Shylock's three hundred and sixty-odd lines, Shakespeare provided material that asks for a whole additional play to work itself out. Granville-Barker perceptively summarizes how much there is in the scene, not sixty lines long, in which Shylock is seen at home:

> The parting with Launcelot: he has a niggard liking for the fellow, is even hurt a little by his leaving, touched in pride, too, and shows it childishly.
>
> > Thou shalt not gormandize
> > As thou hast done with me...
>
> The parting with Jessica, which we of the audience know to be a parting indeed; that constant calling her by name, which tells us of

the lonely man! He has looked to her for everything, has tasked her hard, no doubt; he is her jailer, yet he trusts her, and loves her in his extortionate way. Uneasy stranger that he is within these Venetian gates; the puritan, who, in a wastrel world, will abide by law and prophets!

To have dramatized "he has looked to her for everything, has tasked her hard, no doubt," would have taken Shakespeare far afield indeed from the prodigal story he was concerned with—as far afield as *King Lear*. Yet the suggestion is there. The figure of Shylock is like some secondary figure in a Rembrandt painting, so charged with implied life that one can forget his surroundings. To look sometimes with absorption at the suffering, raging Jew alone is irresistible. But the more one is aware of what the play's whole design is expressing through Shylock, of the comedy's high seriousness in its concern for the grace of community, the less one wants to lose the play Shakespeare wrote for the sake of one he merely suggested.

"These Be the Christian Husbands"

Leslie A. Fiedler

The Merchant of Venice is surely one of the most popular of Shakespeare's works, but by the same token, perhaps, one of the least well understood. The common error which takes the "Merchant" of the title to be Shylock is symptomatic of a whole syndrome of misconceptions about a play which few of us have ever really confronted, so badly is it customarily annotated, taught, and interpreted on the stage and so totally does the Jew now dominate its action. The play has captured our imagination, but Shylock has captured the play, turning, in the course of that conquest, from grotesque to pathetic, from utter alien to one of us.

And why not, since the Jew is, to begin with, an archetype of great antiquity and power, a nightmare of the whole Christian community, given a local habitation and a name by Shakespeare, so apt it is hard to believe that he has not always been called "Shylock," has not always walked the Rialto. The contest between him and the play's other characters—Antonio, for instance, that projection of the author's private distress, or Portia, that not-far-from-standard heroine in male garb—is as unequal as that between mythic Joan and historic Talbot in Henry VI, Part I. Even the sort of transformation he has undergone is not unprecedented in the annals of theater. Molière's "Misanthrope," for example, was converted much more quickly, in less than a generation, rather than over nearly two centuries, from absurd buffoon to sympathetic dissident. But Molière's margin of ambivalence toward Alceste was greater by far than Shakespeare's toward Shylock, and a major revolution in taste and sensibility had begun before he was long dead.

From The Stranger in Shakespeare. © 1972 by Leslie A. Fiedler. Croom Helm, 1973. Originally entitled "The Jew as Stranger: Or 'These be the Christian Husbands.' "

Shakespeare, on the other hand, though not without some prophetic reservations about the wickedness of Jews, had to wait two centuries or more before such reservations had moved from the periphery to the center of the play. To be sure, the original entry in the Stationers' Register for 1598 refers to the play as "a booke of the Marchaunt of Venyce, or otherwise called the Jewe of Venyce"; and by 1701, Lord Lansdowne had quite rewritten it as *The Jew of Venice*. But even at that point, the appeal of Shylock was not so much pathetic as horrific and grotesque. It took three generations of nineteenth-century romantic actors to make the Jew seem sympathetic as well as central, so that the poet Heine, sitting in the audience, could feel free to weep at his discomfiture. The final and irrevocable redemption of Shylock, however, was the inadvertent achievement of the greatest anti-Semite of all time, who did not appear until the twentieth century was almost three decades old. Since Hitler's "final solution" to the terror which cues the uneasy laughter of *The Merchant of Venice*, it has seemed immoral to question the process by which Shylock has been converted from a false-nosed, red-wigged monster (his hair the color of Judas's), half spook and half clown, into a sympathetic victim.

By the same token, it proved possible recently to mount a heterodox production of *The Merchant* as an anti-Semitic play within the larger play of anti-Semitic world history—by enclosing it in a dramatic frame which made clear to the audience that the anti-Semitic travesty they watched was a command performance put on by doomed Jewish prisoners in a Nazi concentration camp. The play within a play turned out in this case to lack a fifth act, since the actor-Shylock "really" stabbed a guard with the knife he whetted on his boot; and that same actor spoke all his speeches in a comic Yiddish accent, except for those scant few lines in which Shakespeare permits the Jew to plead his own humanity. But none of this seems as important finally as its renewed insistence on what everyone once knew: that the play in some sense celebrates, certainly releases ritually, the full horror of anti-Semitism. A Jewish child, even now, reading the play in a class of Gentiles, feels this in shame and fear, though the experts, Gentile and Jewish alike, will hasten to assure him that his responses are irrelevant, even pathological, since "Shakespeare rarely 'takes sides' and it is certainly rash to assume that he here takes an unambiguous stand 'for' Antonio and 'against' Shylock. . . ."

It is bad conscience which speaks behind the camouflage of scholarship, bad conscience which urges us to read Edmund Keane's or Heinrich Heine's Shylock into Shakespeare's lovely but perverse text, as it had almost persuaded us to drop *Henry VI, Part I* (which means, of course, the Pucelle) quite out of the canon. And which finally is worse: to have for so long forgotten Joan, or to persist in misremembering Shylock? In either case, we have, as it were, expurgated

Shakespeare by canceling out or amending the meanings of the strangers at the heart of his plays.

The problem is that both of these particular strangers, the woman and the Jew, embody stereotypes and myths, impulses and attitudes, images and metaphors grown unfashionable in our world. Not that we have been emancipated from those impulses and attitudes, whatever superficial changes have been made in the stereotypes and myths, the images and metaphors which embody them; but we have learned to be ashamed, *officially* ashamed of them at least. And it irks us that they still persist in the dark corners of our hearts, the dim periphery of our dreams. What is demanded of us, therefore, if we would find the real meaning of these plays again, is not so much that we go back into the historical past in order to reconstruct what men once thought of Jews and witches, but rather that we descend to the level of what is most archaic in our living selves and there confront the living Shylock and Joan.

Obviously, it is easier to come to terms with such characters on the "enlightened" margin of Shakespeare's ambivalence. We are pleased to discover how much he is like what we prefer to think ourselves, when, for instance, he allows Shylock a sympathetic apology for himself: "Hath not a Jew eyes? Hath not a Jew hands, organs, dimensions, senses, affections, passions? Fed with the same food, hurt with the same weapons, subject to the same diseases, healed by the same means, warmed and cooled by the same winter and summer as a Christian is? If you prick us, do we not bleed? If you tickle us, do we not laugh? If you poison us, do we not die?"

And we are similarly delighted when Shakespeare lets him for an instant speak out of deep conjugal love: "It was my turquoise, I had it of Leah when I was a bachelor. I would not have given it for a wilderness of monkeys," or when Shakespeare permits him to rehearse the list of indignities he has suffered at Antonio's hands:

> Signior Antonio, many times and oft
> In the Rialto you have rated me
> About my moneys and my usances.
> Still I have borne it with a patient shrug,
> For sufferance is the badge of all our tribe.
> You call me misbeliever, cutthroat dog,
> And spit upon my Jewish gaberdine.

But we must not forget that immediately following that first speech, Shylock is crying "revenge" and vowing that he will practice "villainy," and that scarcely has he spoken the second, when he is dreaming that he will "have the heart of" the Christian merchant. True, he bows and fawns and flatters throughout the third, but in a tone so obviously false, it could fool no one but gullible Antonio. And we would do better, therefore, to face that in ourselves which responds to the negative, which is to say, the stronger, pole of Shakespeare's double view: the uneasiness we feel before those terrible others whom we would but cannot quite believe no longer alien to us and all that we prize.

Women seem to give us even more trouble in this regard than Jews, for all of us have been brainwashed against the "second sex" by poetry of highest power and ribaldry of the widest popular appeal. Surely, then, it is the fear of something responsive in ourselves which makes us unwilling to grant, or quite remember, that Shakespeare, unlike those self-declared defenders of the female from Friedrich Schiller to Jean Anouilh, could really, *really* have traduced the symbol of what is best in woman by mocking the sole saint besides Francis of Assisi to have survived the contempt of a secular age. To this very day, even those who otherwise find the bourgeois apotheosis of women a slight more offensive than outright vilification prefer to think of Shakespeare, quite like the most simpleminded of his nineteenth-century admirers, as the creator of a gallery of good women, or rather of good girls. Did he not, they argue, echoing Mrs. Jameson and Charles Lamb, create the gentle Juliet and Rosalind, as well as the long-suffering Cordelia and Desdemona—and, to be sure, the doughty but delicate Portia herself?

How actresses have always loved that sympathetic part: but not actresses alone, for lovers of Shakespeare still too anti-Semitic to make Shylock into the hero of the play, have given it to Portia, whom they typically remember urging the claims of Christian mercy on the heartless Jew. What they forget is that, like Joan, Portia, too, is an enemy of fathers, and that, like Joan, she puts on male garb; but unlike her French counterpart, she is presented as no threatening stranger. She is rather portrayed as always and everywhere at home: in Belmont, where she recites the litany of her prejudices into the ear of her maid, and in Venice, where, disguised as "a Daniel come to judgment," she acts out in a ritual of Jew-baiting not only her own anti-Semitism, but that of all the other major characters in the play.

She constitutes, in short, the focal center of a play which contains an almost exhaustive catalogue of the stereotypes bred by Elizabethan xenophobia: the stranger-hater *par excellence*, secure in the midst of a protected Establishment. She is as "supersubtle" a Venetian as Desdemona herself, but blonde as the fair youth, which symbolizes her virtue and her worth, not Italian black, which stands for evil, or even Titian red, which would seem ambiguous. And Shakespeare makes it clear that she is not just blonde in appearance like the witch, Joan. Nor is she merely bewigged like those fashionable deceivers granted by the wigmaker's art the "golden . . . dowry of a second head"—on whom Bassanio oddly reflects before opening the right casket and assuring himself her hand, her portrait seeming to him, at the moment of his triumph, to be graced with "a golden mesh to entrap the hearts of men/Faster than gnats in cobwebs."

But where do they come from, these insidious metaphors of rifled graves and insects trapped, so inharmonious with the lovely music of the scene? They represent no *arrière-pensée* of her accepted lover, but rather an irrelevant intrusion of Shakespeare's own marginal ambivalence, the residue of the antifeminist rage that moved him when he wrote *Henry VI* and subverted his attempt this time to write a play in which not the daughter but the father would be a stranger. What Bassanio himself believes, he has unequivocally declared to Antonio on the eve of setting out to woo and win her: "her sunny locks/Hang on her temples like a golden fleece. . . ." And Antonio does not gainsay him. Portia is, in fact, so unchallenged, so secure in the golden heart of her little world, which as long as the play lasts, seems the great world's center, that she can mock every upstart alien who comes in quest of her.

How much like Célimène she sounds, the *médisante* of Molière's *Le Misanthrope*, as one by one she shoots down all the suitor-strangers whom, one by one, Nerissa sets up as targets for the fire of her wit: the horse-mad Neapolitan ("Ay, that's a colt indeed. . . . I am much afeard my lady his mother played false with a smith"); the frowning County Palatine ("He hears merry tales and smiles not. . . . I had rather be married to a death's-head with a bone in his mouth. . . ."); the all-too-adaptable French lord ("God made him, and therefore let him pass for a man. . . . He is every man in no man"); the inarticulate baron of England ("He hath neither Latin, French, nor Italian. . . . He is a proper man's picture, but, alas! who can converse with a dumb show?"); the cowardly Scot (". . . he borrowed a box of the ear of the Englishman and swore he would pay him again when he was able"); the sodden young German ("When he is best, he is a little worse than a man, and when he is worst, he is little better than a beast. . . . set a deep glass of Rhenish wine on the contrary casket, for if the Devil be within and that temptation without, I know he will choose it").

It is not merely that each is in his own way inadequate as a suitor, absurd as a man, but that each, including the Englishman (who proves also a stranger in Belmont, that earthly paradise of absolute belonging), performs his national stereotype—at least so Portia assures us, who never see them—as if on purpose to deserve her scorn. But doing so, they please the audience as well, which knows in advance, but is tickled to be reminded, which foreigner will be mad for horses, which for drink; which will be affected, which supersober, which dumb.

Beyond these half-dozen wooers dismissed, as it were, off stage, we see two actually on scene, in a kind of double introduction to the lucky third, Bassanio. And one of these, as might well be expected in a time when the Armada was still a living memory, is a Spaniard who is largely allowed to damn himself out of his own mouth, talking boastfully of "merit" and "honor," then making, as he must, the wrong choice and exiting with cries of self-reproach. "Did I deserve no more than a fool's head?/Is that my prize?" The second, however, quite unexpectedly turns out to be a Moor, a black man, obviously intended to represent the absolute pole of otherness; and to him Shakespeare gives more space than to any of the other aspirants to Portia's self and fortune, except for Bassanio.

He is mentioned to begin with at the climax of the scene of ticking off the suitors, though, in his case, it is not some stereotypical flaw in character, but his "complexion," which is to say, his skin color, that Portia holds against him, sight unseen: "If he have the condition of a saint and the complexion of a devil, I had rather he should shrive me than wive me." When Morocco actually appears in the next scene, he proves to be, in fact, dignified and sympathetic—a little grandiloquent, perhaps, but not emptily bombastic like the Spaniard. And his first words are a plea against precisely the kind of prejudgment Portia has made. "Mislike me not for my complexion," he says, "The shadowed livery of the burnished sun,/To whom I am a neighbor and near bred. . . ./I would not change this hue,/Except to steal your thoughts, my gentle Queen."

It is one of those noble apologies which Shakespeare permits even the most theoretically ignoble of his outsiders when they speak of what they love, quite like the splendid passage on music and dreams he will bestow on Caliban. Yet most admirers of the play scarcely remember Morocco's words, which seem to contribute nothing to the central encounter between Portia and the Jew. But James Fenimore Cooper, at least, realized the sense in which archetypally the black prince and the Jewish usurer are one, representing the best and worst side of the non-European stranger. And so in *The Last of the Mohicans*, he links them by identifying his noblest savage (Moor plus Jew becoming in his mythic arithmetic Indian) with the former, and his most ignoble with the latter, quoting the black prince's plea on his title page and vindictive tags from Shylock at the head of his bloodiest chapters. Unlike Portia, however, Cooper was willing to treat his Morocco figure with pathos rather than contempt, clearly regretting his failed marriage with a white girl, though not finally permitting it. It is as if he sensed in Shakespeare certain reservations in this regard not shared by his heroine and wanted to make them manifest.

Portia herself, in fact, seems for one moment moved by Morocco's plea to distrust the promptings of her own dearest prejudices and grant that one black on the outside might inwardly be "fair."

> if my father had not scanted me,
> And hedged me by his wit, to yield myself

> His wife who wins me by that means I told you,
> Yourself, renowned Prince, then stood as fair
> As any comer I have looked on yet
> For my affection.

We remember, however, not only what she has said of the Prince earlier but also her opinion of the other suitors so that we catch the equivocation of her phrase: "any . . . I have looked on yet." Moreover, at this point, we have realized that Portia is a courteous liar as well as *médisante*; and yet we surmise beneath her courtly dissimulation the presence in Shakespeare's preconsciousness of possibilities he was later to realize in *Othello*: the accomplished marriage of a "super-subtle" Venetian lady to a noble Moor, with all the attendant joys and woes.

But he will not let it happen here, and, in another (his final) scene, the Prince of Morocco takes and fails the ritual test, choosing the wrong casket because he still must learn that "all that glisters is not gold," and winning as his award not the "angel in a golden bed" he dreamed, but only a *memento mori*, a death's head to remind him that "gilded tombs do worms infold." And once he has left the scene, Portia speaks the concluding couplet, re-echoing the contempt with which she began.

> A gentle riddance. Draw the curtains, go.
> Let all of his complexion choose me so.

She is through now with all her foreign wooers, through with the sham her father's will compels, and ready to accept Bassanio, who alone is really "fair" and of her own kind. She had, in fact, approved of him at first sight, declaring to Nerissa, who mentions him favorably even before the testing of the Spaniard and the Moor, "I remember him well, and I remember him worthy of thy praise."

There is only one stranger in *The Merchant of Venice* whom Portia does not vilify in great detail, and that is—disconcertingly—Shylock, the Jew. But surely this is because Shakespeare assumed that his characteristic faults were already known to everyone, as well as exposed in the plot, and that therefore there was no need to itemize the catalogue: usuriousness, avarice, lust for vengeance, and hostility to music, masquing, and young love. For all of this, in Shakespeare's day, the unmodified generic epithet "Jew" would serve; and so Portia calls Shylock either "Jew" vocative, when they are face to face, or else, in the distancing nominative, "the Jew," turning her back on him to discuss him with her fellow Christians as though he were a creature in another realm of being.

What she leaves unspecified, though not unsuggested, is, in any case, screamed out by Gratiano, who provides throughout the courtroom scene a kind of antiphony of abuse to her pious plain song. "This currish Jew," he amends her unmodified epithet, for instance; and earlier in the scene, he had expanded the metaphor, making a little lyric of his hate.

> Oh, be thou damned, inexecrable dog! . . .
> Thy currish spirit
> Governed a wolf who, hanged for human slaughter,
> Even from the gallows did his fell soul fleet,
> And, whilst thou lay'st in the unhallowed dam
> Infused itself in thee, for thy desires
> Are wolvish, bloody, starved, and ravenous.

Gratiano, indeed, speaks for three: taking away the task of particularized vilification not only from Portia but also from Bassanio, his friend and almost master, to whose not-quite Don Quixote he plays not-quite Sancho Panza. Sometimes Bassanio seems troubled by the manners of his more candid alter ego, warning him at one point that he is "too wild, too rude, and bold of voice." This is, however, while Bassanio is still courting Portia and feels the need of circumspection. And, in any case, he hastens to reassure Gratiano that his excesses are not really evil, only undiplomatic, a premature giveaway of what, beneath the show of courtesy, they both really stand for, what as husbands it will be proper for them both to reveal. Both, finally, are one—along with Lorenzo, Salanio, and Salarino, splittings of a single, charming, feckless, and insolent young man; and their quarrels are family quarrels, arguments about how certain kinds of behavior might appear to outsiders, which "in such eyes as ours appear not faults. . . ."

Gratiano's speech seems in retrospect not just the climax, but the keynote of a whole chorus of anti-Jewish abuse in which many other voices joined: a chorus in which the leitmotif is "dog" and its variations. And Shakespeare, we remember, seems to have been no dog lover at all, reserving his canine metaphors for destructive women, cringing courtiers, and the most treacherous of his villains. Antonio himself has used that word in insult before the action of the play begins, as we learn from Shylock, in whom it continues to rankle. He can hardly keep his tongue away from it, in fact, referring to it over and over in his first conversation with Antonio. "You call me misbeliever, cutthroat dog. . . . And foot me as you spurn a stranger cur. . . . "Hath a dog money? Is it possible/A cur can lend three thousand ducats?' . . . another time you called me dog. . . ." The effect is odd, finally, Shylock's intended ironies cutting the wrong way, so that the audience ends feeling he is self-condemned, branded a "dog" out of his own mouth, rather than out of Antonio's, who on scene only answers quietly, "I am as like to call thee so again. . . ."

Nor does Shylock leave it at that, insisting later, when he has Antonio at his mercy, "Thou call'dst me dog before thou hadst a cause,/But since I am a dog, beware my fangs." This time, Antonio proves as good as his word, even upping the ante from "dog" to "wolf," as he addresses the court. "You may as well use questions with the wolf,/Why he hath made the ewe bleat for the lamb. . . ." It must have been an especially effective epithet at the moment, reminding Shakespeare's audience of the pun implicit in the name "Lopez" or read into it at least by those eager to make clear how appropriately it was borne by the Spanish-Jewish doctor to Elizabeth, who had just been executed for treason.

Meanwhile, Salanio and Salarino — those echoers of fashion and each other — take up the theme, referring to "the dog Jew" and "the most impenetrable cur." Indeed, the range of insults for Jews seems pitifully limited in Venice. The Duke himself, it is true, manages "stony adversary" and "inhuman wretch"; but generally, if it is not "dog," it is "Devil." So Salanio once more speaks of "the Devil . . . in the likeness of a Jew." Even that dullest of Shakespearean clowns, Launcelot Gobbo, describes his old master at one point as "the very Devil incarnal"; and the lovely apostate Jessica makes the same point by implication, speaking of how she found "our house is hell. . . ."

Like all forms of obscenity, the abuse bred by prejudice is notably monotonous, so that reading over the anti-Semitic tirades of *The Merchant of Venice*, one thinks somehow of Bédier's comment after years of editing the fabliaux (those rhymed dirty jokes of the Middle Ages, themselves based on vilification of women and clerics) about "the incredible monotony of the human obscene." There are, to be sure, a wide range of possible inflections of obscenity; and Shakespeare's play constitutes, as it were, a little anthology of these: the note of dignified contempt in Antonio, Bassanio, and Portia; the note of tender self-hatred in Jessica; the note of endearing imprecision in Gobbo; the note of passionate self-indulgence in Gratiano, becoming secondhand chic in Salanio and Salarino. It is, however, the sense of a repetitiveness verging on obsession which remain with us — revealing finally how deep the roots of anti-Semitic horror go at all levels of the society which Shakespeare portrays.

And, indeed, the clue to what lies at those roots is provided by the very terms of abuse; for "devil" plus "dog" or "wolf" add up to "ogre," a symbol of great mythic potency: the male equivalent of the witch-mother, and like her associated with the murder or eating of children. The witch, as we have seen, represents in one of her aspects (appearing also in Shakespeare as the witch-daughter) the evil mother, who cannot bear to leave alive outside herself the maturing daughter whose beauty she feels a challenge to her fading charms. To think, for instance, of the wicked Queen in *Cymbeline* is to be reminded of the stepmothers and witches, sometimes split and sometimes joined, in such ancient tales as "Hansel and Gretel" or "Snow White." In Shakespeare, however, another dimension is added, since his cruelest mothers dream rape rather than cannibalism, whetting the lust of their spoiled sons against the hated stepdaughters.

The ogre, on the other hand, stands for the evil father, who seeks to swallow down his son, thus ingesting the male strength he has sired lest it destroy and succeed him. But in his war against time, the ogre-father, unwilling to yield his privileges to anyone, seeks also to become his own son-in-law by keeping his natural daughter for himself. The twin threat of the ogre is, therefore, cannibalism and incest, cannibalism to the son and incest to the daughter. But this constitutes a double process of life-denial which, archetypally, is endless, since even the sons born of the daughter must be eaten, the daughters of the daughter possessed before they fall into the hands of the other—and so (ogres being immortal) with the children of those children, and their descendants to the end of time.

Insofar as the *The Merchant of Venice* tells the story of the "merry bond," it is concerned with the threat of the ogre to the son. Insofar as it tells that of the three caskets, it deals with his threat to the daughter. And in both, it evokes archetypal patterns which lie far beneath Shakespeare's conscious mythologizing of his own life, patterns that came to him, as they continue to come to us, out of sources deeper than literature or waking experience—those old wives' tales we can scarcely distinguish from our dreams. In those tales and dreams, creatures much like Shylock, though still without a proper name, not even "Jew," rise to confront us. Half devil and half wolf they seem, which is to say, like the Devil of popular imagination, not-quite-humans in almost human form and, like the wolves of travelers' chronicles, eaters of human flesh.

It is the Duke of Venice who sums up the first aspect of Shylock, calling him "a stony adversary" (but the Hebrew word for "adversary" is "Satan") and "an inhuman wretch"; and doing so, he has in effect, already condemned him by finding him nonhuman, something else. Similarly, Gratiano qualifies him as a dog run wild ("wolvish, bloody, starved, and ravenous"), though it is Shylock himself who seems earlier to have insisted on making the cannibalistic nature of his hunger for human flesh quite clear. "I will feed fat the ancient grudge I bear him," he declares of Antonio near the beginning of the play; and the metaphor is reinforced a few lines later when he remarks, even more inadvertently it would seem, to Antonio, who has just entered, "Your Worship was the last man in our mouths." Before the scene is through, he has also said to Bassanio, brushing aside his worries about the pound of flesh his friend has offered to forfeit should he fail to meet his loan, "A pound of man's flesh taken from a man/Is not so estimable, profitable neither,/As the flesh of muttons, beefs, or goats. . . ."

It seems overreading, perhaps, to insist that some notion of eating human flesh is already implicit in such a casual butcher's list. Yet two acts later, that shadowy implication becomes an explicitly cannibalistic metaphor when Shylock, in response to Salarino's query, "Why, I am sure if he forfeit, thou wilt not take his flesh. What's that good for?," answers, "To bait fish withal. If it will feed nothing else, it will feed my revenge." And this, the grimmest of these threats, it should be noticed, is followed almost immediately by the noblest of his apologies, which asks, among other things, if a Jew is not "fed with the same food . . . as a Christian is?"

But, of course, Shylock does not actually eat Antonio, does not even really want to eat him, except maybe in dreams, even though he does want him dead, feeling him—along with all his friends and doubles—as rebellious Christian sons, who, in seeking to destroy Judaism, have turned against the father of Jews and Christians alike, the patriarch, Abraham. As a matter of fact, even metaphors of eating disappear from the text in act 4, which marks the climax and end of the bond plot, being replaced by the image of the threatening father with a knife, a special variant of the ogre archetype derived not from fairy tales, but precisely from the story of Abraham and Isaac in the Scriptures of the Jews.

Meanwhile, both father-son myths are being hard beset by a cognate myth, known in its folk-tale form as "the ogre's daughter": the story of a girl who betrays her own inhuman father, sometimes letting him be killed, always permitting the stealing of his treasure—and all for the sake of a human hero, with whom she afterward tries to flee back to his world. It is a tale best remembered these days as the Grimm brothers have reproduced it in "Jack and the Beanstalk," in which version the daughter has been transformed into the wife of the giant cannibal, to obscure the incestuous nature of their connection. But in *The Merchant of Venice*, the archetypal daughter remains at least a daughter, though the incest motif is camouflaged in other ways.

Two ogre's daughters, in fact, two female betrayers of the father, appear in this play, whose dreamlike logic, having already splintered the human rival to the monster-father into several fragments, also splits the treacherous daughter into Portia and Jessica. Each functions, as the names indicate, in a separate mythological world: the one classical or Greco-Roman, the other biblical or Hebreo-Christian—the two complementary traditions, in short, which made the mind of the Renaissance.

It is easy to identify Jessica as the ogre's daughter, considerably less so to realize that Portia plays a similar part. But a clue is given early by a reference to Shakespeare's favorite source book of classical mythology, Ovid's *Metamorphoses*. Toward the end of the first scene of act 1, Bassanio, pressing Antonio for a loan so that he can court Portia in proper style, passes from praise of her blonde beauty to the evocation of a mythological parallel to his quest.

> And her sunny locks
> Hang on her temples like a golden fleece,
> Which makes her seat of Belmont Colchos' strond,
> And many Jasons come in quest of her.
> O my Antonio, had I but the means
> To hold a rival place with one of them.

Moreover, after Bassanio has got "the means"—borrowed for him by Antonio on the security of "the bond"—and has chosen the proper casket of the three, Gratiano completes the identification with the myth of Colchos by crowing, "We are the Jasons, we have won the fleece."

But if Bassanio is archetypally Jason, then Portia must be Medea, which is to say, "the cunning one," a witch, however favorable she may be to the hero, and, as a witch, an enemy to fathers. It is a role in which it is hard to imagine Portia, and yet there are close analogies between her actions and those of her ancient prototype. Medea's own father, Aeëtes, had set for Jason a triple task which seemed impossible to achieve; but already in love with him, Medea helped him pass the test by magic. And just so, Portia, by the only kind of witchcraft Shakespeare will permit in *The Merchant of Venice*, the spell of song, helps Bassanio solve the triple riddle posed by the "will" of her dead father.

It is well to be clear about the nature of the task Portia's would-be husbands were asked to perform, as well as the penalties imposed for failing it. Nerissa describes it first as a "lottery that he hath devised in these three chests of gold, silver, and lead—whereof who chooses his meaning chooses you. . . ." And the Prince of Morocco clarifies the matter further by reading aloud the riddling inscriptions on all three.

> The first, of gold, who this inscription bears,
> "Who chooseth me shall gain what many men desire."
> The second, silver, which this promise carries,
> "Who chooseth me shall get as much as he deserves."
> This third, dull lead, with warning all as blunt,
> "Who chooseth me must give and hazard all he hath."

But it is left to Portia to explain the penalty for choosing wrong, which is, "Never to speak to lady afterward/In way of marriage."

The triple riddle, with its three clichés, seems not especially hard to solve; though behind it readers have always sensed a more absolute enigma, the riddle of the riddle, which Shakespeare seems not himself to have quite understood. Many famous puzzle-solvers, including Sigmund Freud, have tried to guess the meaning of the three caskets. Some suggest that all three represent female sexuality, which to the "wrong man" means death; some, that, like the three daughters in *King Lear* or such fairy tales as "Cinderella," they are meant to illustrate nothing more recondite than the Christian paradox that the last shall be first. Others, however, have suggested that they are therapeutic rather than homiletic, a parable meant to exorcise the fantasy of preadolescents that their unworthy siblings are preferred and they are cast off like hated stepchildren.

In *The Merchant of Venice*, however, that parable blurs into the even more terrifying tale of the sleeping princess, who can be awakened only by her lover's kiss, once he has penetrated the maze in which her father's possessiveness has immured her. And that maze, like the riddle which is its alternative form (surely this is what the ban on future marriages signifies), threatens castration to those who do not make it through.

Being, however, witch as well as bewitched, Medea as well as *belle au bois dormante*, Portia provides her lover with the clue he needs to find her and avoid unmanning. It is all there in the "magic" she has sung to him.

> Tell me where is fancy bred,
> Or in the heart or in the head?
> How begot, how nourished?
> > Reply, reply.
> It is engendered in the eyes,
> With gazing fed, and fancy dies
> In the cradle where it lies.
> > Let us all ring fancy's knell.
> > I'll begin it. — Ding, dong, bell.

Not only the spell of the music, which, as everywhere in Shakespeare, resolves discord and dispels terror, but the words, too, do the trick: the reiterated end rhymes in "ed" of the first stanza, echoed in the word "fed" in the very midst of the second, and reinforced by the allusion to death on which the whole closes. They move Bassanio to make — on the rim of consciousness where the "magical" occurs — associations with the unspoken words "dead" and "lead" and thus to realize that the casket in which his golden girl is "locked" is a coffin, where she lies, as if wrapped in lead, until he revives her. "Turn you where your lady is," reads the "gentle scroll" inside the leaden box, "and claim her with a loving kiss." Only so can "the will of a living daughter" triumph over the "will of a dead father" (the play on the word "will" hints at the theme of incest foiled), and only so can Jason have, as the Medea archetype demands, the Golden Fleece.

But like Medea, Portia is involved with more fathers than one — with three in fact. Her ancient prototype had first renewed Aeson, the good father of her lover, Jason, then tricked to his death Pelias, his wicked uncle, which is to say in archetypal terms, his bad father. And so Portia, reversing the order, first redeems (or seems to, there being a quibble here) Bassanio's good father, Antonio, who declares in gratitude, "Sweet lady, you have given me life and living," then tricks into a catastrophe as near to death as the ground rules of comedy will allow, the bad father, Shylock. "You take my life/When you do take the means whereby I live," the Jew declares before his final exit, then dies to the action as his intended victim moves toward the happy ending he would have foiled. Portia, however, never overtly makes the identification of herself with Medea— in part, perhaps, because Shakespeare consciously was reluctant to draw a parallel between so sympathetic a heroine and the descendant of the archwitch Circe.

He therefore portrays her as, in her own eyes at least, the passive victim of one generation's male villainy awaiting deliverance by the male heroism of another; though this completely contradicts what happens in the play. "Go, Hercules!" she cries to the quite un-Herculean Bassanio as he stands musing over the three caskets. "Live thou, I live. With much more dismay/I view the fight than thou that makest the fray." That we do not feel the whole scene as travesty is a tribute to Portia's magic and her maker's, for if Bassanio's view of himself as Jason is absurd, her own self-image is doubly so. Jason, at least, depended for his triumphs on the women who loved him, as Bassanio depends on Portia and on the "woman's part" in Antonio; but the fights of Hercules were real and bloody and won without the help of anything but his own miraculous strength.

Nonetheless, thinking of her lover thus enables Portia to see herself as "the virgin tribute paid by howling Troy/To the sea monster," which is to say, to claim archetypal kinship with Hesione, whom Hercules rescued after the treachery or cowardice of her untrustworthy father had condemned her to death. "I stand for sacrifice," she declares, not only making clear her conviction that her father's last will has condemned her to a living death but also identifying herself with all other girls offered up by kingly fathers for great causes which those daughters neither understood nor wished to. Iphigenia comes especially to mind, bound to the altar by Agamemnon eager to be off to Troy, that archetype of the Hellenic world closest to the Hebrew myth of the sacrifice of Isaac.

But Jessica, the Jew's daughter, toward the close of her moonlit duet with Lorenzo at the opening of act 5 names the name that neither Bassanio nor Portia had dared utter. Theirs is the first happy ending we are shown, after Shylock's disappearance from the stage, but it is qualified by a gentle melancholy which impels them to linger over the sorrows of lovers long dead as well as to utter presentiments about their own future. Such melancholy is not rare in this bitter comedy, in which Antonio enters confessing that "such a want-wit sadness makes of me/That I have much ado to know myself." And Portia's first words are:

"By my troth, Nerissa, my little body is aweary of this great world." But its causes are elsewhere more clearly specified. Portia is sad because she fears she will never marry; and Antonio, because he knows he never can. But what moves Jessica in the first hours of her honeymoon to recite a litany of mythic tales from Ovid and Chaucer all involving death and betrayal?

It is Lorenzo who begins by invoking Troilus at the moment when he "sighed his soul toward the Grecian tents,/Where Cressid lay that night"—lay, as his listeners know, with false Diomede. But it is Jessica who says, bringing the mythic catalogue to a close:

> In such a night
> Medea gathered the enchanted herbs
> That did renew old Aeson.

She evokes, to be sure, the most benign of all the achievements of "the crafty one," an act of white magic; but doing so, reminds us of the darker aspects of Medea's story: her betrayal of two fathers and Jason's deception of her. Jessica, however, is no Medea figure, though she has begun by gilding herself "with some moe ducats" stolen from her father for the sake of her lover, who, remembering that moment, says:

> In such a night
> Did Jessica steal from the wealthy Jew,
> And with an unthrift love did run from Venice.

But she has been purged by suffering to a touching gentleness and leaves the scene no witch at all, only a fearful wife. She has been transformed from the Ovidian version of the ogre's daughter into a variant medieval in origin and Christian in essence: the Jew's daughter, or more precisely, the Jew's faithless daughter, which is to say, God's faithful servant.

The archetype of the menacing Jewish father with the knife and the blessed apostasy of his daughter is created by grafting onto a pre-Christian folktale elements derived from the official mythology of the Christian church, though much altered in the course of popular transmission. More specifically, it represents an attempt to translate into mythological form the dogmatic compromise by which Christianity managed to make the New Testament its Scripture without surrendering the Old, and in the course of doing so, worked out ways of regarding the Jews simultaneously as the ultimate enemy, the killers of Christ, and the chosen people, with whom God made the covenant, the bond (this is the meaning of "testament"), under which all who believe in Jesus as the Christ are saved.

At the heart of the Old Testament, however, stands the figure of the patriarch with whom that covenant was first sealed, and who, for its sake, first cir-

cumcised his son (as his heirs under the new covenant do not), then tied him
to the altar as a sacrifice. "And Abraham stretched forth his hand, and took the
knife to slay his son." It is an image which has haunted Europe for nearly two
millennia: the original Jew, bearded and ancient, raising aloft the threatening
blade as Isaac, whom the rabbis taught was thirty years old or more, but whom
the imagination of Christianity has made a child, watches from the altar in sub-
missive silence. But Abraham is connected also with the New Testament, the
new covenant, in which patriarchal rigor is replaced by maternal mercy; the symbol
of that mercy, Mary herself, on learning her destiny, evokes his name. According
to Saint Luke, at least, that chosen Jewish maiden, standing belly to belly with
her long-barren cousin, Elizabeth, both of them miraculously pregnant, says,
"My soul doth magnify the Lord. . . . For he has regarded the low estate of his
handmaiden. . . . He hath holpen his servant Israel, in remembrance of his mercy;
As he spake to our fathers, to Abraham, and to his seed for ever." That is to
say, she declares herself a daughter of Abraham, an inheritor of the covenant,
and in due course, circumcises her son on the eighth day, as the first Jewish
father did his.

Even those Christians with little or no knowledge of the web of exegesis
that was spun around these texts—beginning with Paul's Epistle to the Romans
("to the end the promise might be sure to all the seed; not to that only which
is of the law, but to that also which is of the faith of Abraham; who is the
father of us all. . . .")—have been dimly aware of their filial relationship to
Judaism. Yet to such minds, the myth of Mary's virginity seems to mean that
though herself in one sense Jewish, she does not belong to her Jewish father,
much less to his impotent surrogate, her Jewish husband, but only to her Christian
sons. Archetypally, that is to say, she exists as no one's wife, but as an eternal daughter-mother, purged at once of the evil embodied in her ancestry and
in the act by which all humans are conceived—a being utterly female without
being human: Pearl of Great Price, Rose without Thorns, Burning Bush, Star
of the Sea. So sublimated, however, the female principle cannot be imagined
as acting in human affairs, only on them; and this posed a problem for the earliest
Christian mythmakers.

In the first Christian folk tales embodying such myths, therefore, only the
evil Jewish father and the Gentile child he threatens really exist in time and on
earth; the Jewish mother-daughter intervenes from the eternal heavens. The tale,
for instance, which Chaucer puts into the mouth of his Prioress is typical in
this regard, representing, indeed, the form in which the archetype possessed the
mind of Europe for almost a thousand years, beginning, it would seem, around
A.D. 500, and reaching the peak of its popularity between 1200 and 1400. At
this point, the original anti-Semitic child-murder story—born of the confluence

in the popular mind of much half-remembered scriptural stuff: the sacrifice of Isaac, the massacre of Hebrew infants by the Pharaoh, the death of the Egyptian first-born, the slaughter of the innocents, the execution of Christ at the high priest's instigation—had been transformed into a "miracle of the Virgin." And as such it enjoyed its greatest vogue. Industrious Chaucer scholars have discovered nearly thirty contemporary analogues, and in Chaucer's own retelling, along with William Wordsworth's modern Englishing, it continues still to charm and terrify quite-sophisticated readers.

In *The Prioress's Tale*, the archetypal calamity befalls a seven-year-old Gentile boy, whose way to and from school takes him every day through the town's "Jewerye." At first, he is not molested or menaced, until he learns from an older friend a hymn in praise of the Virgin, *Alma redemptoris*, which he insists on practicing aloud under the very windows of the Jews. And they are so infuriated by this tribute to an apostate daughter of Abraham that they, prompted by the "serpent Sathanas" in their hearts, hire a Jewish murderer, who with the archetypal knife cuts the boy's throat to the "nekke boon." To conceal the crime, they throw his body in a privy, where "thise Jewes purgen hire entraille"; but he continues to sing his song, since God's Mother, whom he has adored, has put a magic "greyn" upon his tongue that will not let him cease until his corpse is found and his assailants apprehended, torn apart by wild horses, and then hanged.

Those assailants are described as Jews, both the actual assassin and the cabal of plotters who hired him, but nowhere are we reminded that "Cristes mooder" was a Jew as well; for the point of the tale, like that of the courtroom scene in *The Merchant of Venice*, is to make the symbolic equations: Jew equals murderer; Christian equals "welle of mercy." And to clinch the point, the final stanza evokes a more recent incident in England itself, the murder of the boy Hugh of Lincoln, whose case—true to myth, however fictional—is also memorialized in a child's ballad.

> O yonge Hugh of Lyncoln, slayn also
> With cursed Jewes, as it is notable,
> For it is but a litel while ago,
> Preye eek for us, we synful folk unstable,
> That, of his mercy, God so merciable
> On us his grete mercy multiplie,
> For reverence of his mooder Marie.

In that ballad, however, an actual Jewish girl appears—"The Jewe's Daughter," in fact, of its subtitle—though only as the accomplice of her father, the beautiful bait in his terrible trap.

By the time Shakespeare was dreaming Shylock and Jessica, there had begun to grow both in him and in his audience a longing—unsatisfied by either *The Prioress's Tale* or "Sir Hugh, or The Jewe's Daughter"—for a representation of the female principle in Jewish form more human than the Blessed Virgin, yet, unlike the Jew's daughter of the ballad, benign and on their side: a good Jewish daughter of a bad Jewish father, in short. And Shakespeare's Jessica is the first distinguished embodiment of this secularized archetype after Abigail, daughter of Barabas, in Marlowe's *The Jew of Malta*, who, however, flees to a convent rather than a Christian husband.

The Jewish angel of mercy brought down from heaven has flourished ever since in English and American literature: as the Rebecca of Scott's *Ivanhoe*, for instance; the Ruth of Melville's long poem *Clarel*; even as Trilby, perhaps, in the popular novel called by her name. In deciding the fate of such latter-day descendants of Jessica, however, their authors have tended to follow Scott's model rather than Shakespeare's; which is to say, they have not finally allowed the marriages with the Gentile heroes to take place, no matter how angelic the heroines may be. In all such writers, however, the steep contrast between father and daughter, which Shakespeare and Marlowe sensed as central to the myth, continues to prevail; and what inhibits the possibility of the happy ending is the shift of anti-Semitism in the nineteenth century from a religious to a "racist" base, as science ousts theology. Yet no racist's Jew is more terrible, more absolute in his obduracy than Shylock—unmatched even by Marlowe's contemporary Jew of Malta, who seems too bad to be true, a caricature of the fears that fostered him. Among later nightmare versions of the Jew, Dickens's Fagin comes closest in archetypal power to Shakespeare's Shylock, though he moves through a fable without daughters, only adopted sons. Still, in him the smiler with a knife returns, disguised as a nineteenth-century English fence, but essentially the specter that had haunted Christendom for centuries in all its authentic horror and splendor and absurdity.

Shylock, on the other hand, is portrayed as a "usurer," a lender of money on interest rather than a receiver of stolen goods, as is appropriate to his time. In point of fact, Jews (though not only Jews) were usurers during the many hundreds of years when they were forbidden by Christian law to practice other trades and professions. But Jews alone were identified as usurers pure and simple, rather than as men who, like the Medici or dukes of Norwich, happened to have grown rich in that theoretically forbidden way. Even in Chaucer's poem, the offhand equation Jew equals usurer is assumed, an axiom from which the corollary follows that Jew equals killer: "a Jewerye,/Sustened by a lord of that contree/For foule usure and lucre of vileynye. . . ."

But there is mythological as well as historical justification for this, since archetypally the Jew does not exist at all, not even for himself, until he has made his covenant with God, a bond or contract involving promises to be kept, with rewards and penalties contingent on their performance or nonperformance — quite like a promissory note signed to secure a loan. The link, that is to say, which joins together scriptural and legal notions of the bond, identifying both with nascent capitalism, exists in fact and fantasy alike; and this connection Shakespeare exploits with great effect, moving from market place to the Bible and back again in the exchanges between Antonio and Shylock at the beginning of the play.

There is no meeting of minds between these two, who confront each other from across a time barrier which is also the border between two mythologies: the Jewish merchant already in a mercantile future, in which God's promise to his people will be ironically fulfilled; the Christian merchant clinging to a feudal past, in which that people was excluded and despised. Shylock begins by raging to himself against Antonio, who "in low simplicity/. . . lends out money gratis and brings down/The rate of usance. . . ." What is an accusation for him, however, is a boast for Antonio, who says, entering, "I neither lend nor borrow,/By taking nor by giving of excess. . . ."

Yet the importunities of Bassanio have forced him to ask for a loan on Shylock's customary terms, and Shylock welcomes the opportunity to give a little lecture on the propriety of interest, with appropriate scriptural citations. All this proves too much for Antonio, however, who, whatever necessity compels, would like to believe that piety is on his side; and so he interrupts Shylock, crying out:

> Was this inserted to make interest good?
> Or is your gold and silver ewes and rams?

Shylock answers, dryly, "I cannot tell. I make it breed as fast." But his little joke inspires only horror in Antonio, who, quite orthodoxly, considers thriving on "a breed for barren metal" a sin against human industry, nature, and ultimately God himself.

All this, however thematically important, turns out to be beside the immediate point, since this time Shylock wants no "usance" at all to be written into the bond, only (in what he calls "a merry sport") a promise that if repayment is not made on time, Antonio will forfeit "an equal pound/Of your fair flesh, to be cut off and taken/In what part of your body pleaseth me." And with this shift from "barren metal" to living flesh, we have moved back to that other, more archaic set of associations with the bond, moved back to circumcision and Father Abraham.

Long before the old Jew with the knife has been turned into the usurer, the precapitalist threatening disruption to the medieval *oecumene*, he was felt as a menace to something dearer to the deep psyche than the priority of land over money, a threat to manhood itself. Certainly, with the coming of full capitalism, an economy in which everyone from the great industrialist to the housewife with her small savings in the bank profited by interest, the terror of the Jew is not allayed; and that terror has survived into the era of postcapitalism in countries where the state has become the only usurer.

The Protocols of the Elders of Zion, the Beiliss case, the Nazi extermination and calumnies of Streicher, the continuing campaigns of vilification and persecution in Poland, the Soviet Union, and the Arab world, as well as in the more genteel West—these represent an unbroken, perhaps endless, chain. (The false accusation of child murder against Mendel Beiliss in the year 1911 shook the entire liberal world in those now irrecoverable days before Hitler when single victims still somehow managed to count. Beiliss was finally exonerated but his name has become proverbial, in the Jewish community at least.) Even yet the ghost of Father Abraham has not been laid, and Father Abraham, in the nightmares of the simple Christian, who does not awake from them simply by ceasing to go to church, has become the castrating papa: the performer of the first circumcision and the would-be, the almost-sacrificer of the son blending into a single figure forever whetting on his boot sole a knife to cut away the chunk of living flesh he claims for his patriarchal due.

Small wonder, then, that everywhere in the popular Christian literature of Shakespeare's day—in the Gesta Romanorum, Il Percorone of Ser Giovanni Fiorentino, Anthony Munday's Zelauto, the ballad of Gernutus, the Jew of Venice, even in Alexandre Sylvaynes' Orator (presumably a collection of moral debates rather than of fiction)—the mythic theme recurs, and that all these books not written originally in English were translated to feed the hunger which Shakespeare's and Marlowe's Jewish plays, as well as Gosson's lost The Jew, tried to appease.

Tales of flesh promised or surrendered for a boon are found in the myths of all times and places, and in the Christian era they are often associated with witchcraft, as in the case of Joan of Arc, who, according to Shakespeare, declares to her familiars, "I'll lop a member off and give it to you. . . . My body shall/Pay recompense if you will grant my suit," then goes on to promise even more, "Then take my soul, my body, soul and all. . . ." More typically, however, the Renaissance separated the offer of the soul from the bond of flesh, associating the first exclusively with Satan, the second with that minor devil, the Jew. Both female witchcraft and Jewish usury, on the other hand, reflect the male Gentile's fear of loss of potency; and, in this sense, the paranoia behind the myth of the merry bond, like that which motivates the myth of the satanic pact, reveals a hidden truth, since paranoiacs, as Freud once disconcertingly reminded us, never entirely lie. Judaism *has* unmanned the Gentile world, insofar as Jewish morality, transmitted via Christianity, limits and controls the free sexuality presumably enjoyed by men in pre-Christian Europe. It is that morality which the pagan undermind of Europe imagines holding a knife to its genitals, and the consequent resentment which male Europeans feel, but cannot confess, against their own church they project back upon the mythic founder of it all: old Father Abraham.

That Shakespeare identified Shylock with the archetypal Abraham there seems no doubt, for he puts the patriarchal name into the merchant's mouth right from the start. "This Jacob from our holy Abram was." Shylock reminds Antonio in the midst of his casuistical defense of usury; and a little later, just after proposing the merry bond, he cries out in ironical dismay, "O Father Abram, what these Christians are. . . ." The phrase prepares for the later, more serious cry, "These be the Christian husbands," which is itself followed by a last reference to Jessica, whose name was surely suggested to Shakespeare by the Iscah of Genesis, daughter of Haran, who is brother to Abraham. "I have a daughter," Shylock says, "Would any of the stock of Barabas/Had been her husband rather than a Christian!" Shakespeare had found the name Barabas in the same New Testament context from which Marlowe borrowed it for his Jew, taking it (since he did not know its etymological significance, "son of the father") to mean "thief" and "murderer," the murderer, in fact, whom the perfidious Jews chose for Passover amnesty in preference to Jesus.

At this point, Shylock seems more Jephthah than Abraham, the daughter's enemy rather than the son's, though Jessica stands not for "sacrifice" (in the end she gains all, loses nothing), but for everything in the Judaic tradition which represents gentleness as opposed to rigor, love as opposed to justice, the right hand as opposed to the left, and as such is thought to be worthy of good fortune in the Christian world. "Gentle Jew," she is called in one place, and the pun on "Gentile" is intended. There is, therefore, a kind of truth in Salarino's mocking response to Shylock: "There is more difference between thy flesh and hers than between jet and ivory, more between your bloods than there is between red wine and Rhenish."

But it is also true, as Jessica herself insists to Launcelot Gobbo, that however alien "to his manners," she is undeniably a "daughter to his blood." And when that clown asks her to hope that she is "not the Jew's daughter," she can only answer in melancholy jest, "That were a kind of bastard hope, indeed. So the sins of my mother should be visited upon me." No, her only legitimate "hope" is to be saved by her husband, who, as she tells Gobbo, "hath made me a Christian"; which is to say, she can only be saved by elopement and apostasy, by what must seem to her father filial rebellion: "My own flesh and blood to rebel!" To rebel against a very devil, however, can only be construed as virtuous, even if that devil is a father and one thinks, as Shakespeare did, that filial impiety is among the worst of sins.

The myth of the ogre's daughter, in any case, provided Shakespeare with a way out of the trap into which he felt himself betrayed each time he turned to comedy, which in his time—and always, it would seem, at its most popular—demands at its close marriage, which means the abandonment of fathers by daughters they are apt to love too well. But (as in *Henry VI, Part I* and the *Sonnets*) Shakespeare's personal mythology considered not marriage but male friendship the redeeming sentimental relationship and the denial of the father the equivalent of damnation. Once he had abandoned the relatively loose, essentially nonmythic structures of the sonnet sequence and chronicle play—structures which in themselves imposed no archetypal overview—he found himself, therefore, in trouble. Especially the New Comic mode, that benign version of the Oedipal conflict inherited from Plautus and Terence, implied (as Northrop Frye has convincingly demonstrated) a kind of overmyth, to which the submyths implicit in particular plots had to be accommodated.

It is fascinating to watch Shakespeare, from the time of *Love's Labor's Lost*, struggling against the mythological imperative that boy must get girl and that the older generation must be frustrated in desires which at first Shakespeare does not even suspect may be incestuous. In that freest of his early comedies, he begins, as we have already observed, by subverting the dream of a homosexual utopia so that, it would appear (though he supplies in the text reasons biological and theological as well), the conventions of New Comic theater can be honored. But he cannot quite compel himself to end in a quadruple marriage. The death of a king intervenes, the "will of a dead father" inhibiting the intended course of four courtships; and, as Berowne mournfully declares: "Our wooing doth not end like an old play./Jack hath not Jill."

Later, his inherited comic plots no longer permit so evasive an un-ending, and he provides for his audiences the scenes of love triumphant which they demand—establishing, however, certain ground rules of his own to mitigate the Oedipal implications he could not abide. Though daughters can sometimes deceive fathers with impunity in his comedies, sons never can; nor can wives ever betray their husbands—only seem to. Yet even inside these self-imposed parameters, he appears not to have felt quite at ease, haunted always by the sense that those who defied their fathers even in love's name deserved to die. The archetypal story corresponding to that sense he found, like so much else, in Ovid: in the tale of Pyramus and Thisbe, who, deceiving their parents, found only death by moonlight, executing themselves as if in error, but really in response to exigencies they never understand. It is a myth which obsessed Shakespeare throughout the early part of his career, apt to surface in his mind whenever he imagined, for whatever reason, a scene lit only by the moon.

In *Titus Andronicus*, for instance, the first and most improbable allusion occurs; Martius, finding the bloody corpse of Bassianus, is moved to say, "So pale did shine the moon on Pyramus/When he by night lay bathed in maiden blood." The last is put into the mouth of Jessica, in an idyllic scene whose opening words are, "The moon shines bright."

> In such a night
> Did Thisbe fearfully o'ertrip the dew,
> And saw the lion's shadow ere himself,
> And ran dismayed away.

And in the most moon-drenched of all Shakespeare's plays, *A Midsummer Night's Dream*, the Ovidian story of bootlegged love come to grief is travestied by bumpkins all the way to its bitter end, though "Moonshine" through some confusion has left the scene early and "Thisby" must, therefore, kill herself in the dark.

> Come blade, my breast imbrue.
> And, farewell, friends.
> Thus Thisby ends.
> Adieu, adieu, adieu.

Laughing, we do not notice that meanwhile, in the main plot, Hermia, who has like Thisbe defied her father, survives the madness of the night to win his forgiveness and her own true love. And this, indeed, may have been Shakespeare's intent in making a burlesque of Ovid's tale the play within the play.

How different the effect in *Romeo and Juliet*, in which the Ovidian myth, with little changed except the names, becomes the main plot, the tragedy of "star-crossed lovers" — or rather, a foiled comedy, a comedy gone wrong. Those who do not understand all this worry much about why the two lovers have to die, Shakespeare having perversely (they argue) blurred the motivation provided by his Italian and his English sources. It is, however, the myth which kills them finally: the myth misunderstood by those who first turned Pyramus and Thisbe to Romeo and Juliet, but understood by Ovid long before and by his Elizabethan alter ego afterward, the myth which insists, in New Comedy's despite, that every marriage makes a father weep and that for those tears the price is blood.

With *The Merchant of Venice*, however, Shakespeare seems to have exorcised that archetypal ghost at last by substituting for Ovid's bloody fable the happy-ending folktale of the ogre's daughter, in which the death of Thisbe becomes a cadence in a lovers' serenade. In this play, therefore, Jack hath his Jill three times over, as Shakespeare lets his three pairs of lovers move inexorably toward marriage, only insisting, by way of ritual purgation, that each of the three girls first pass as a boy. But how perfunctory the sex-shifting remains, perhaps because Shakespeare is still scarcely aware of what it means or, maybe, rather because he wants this time for once to have his women triumph *as women*, though in boy's clothing. There seems, indeed, something almost willfully perverse, even self-punishing, about the conclusion of *The Merchant of Venice*, a sense of the poet grimly denying the impulse in himself which had resisted New Comedy. It is almost as if he had lost his original innocence, realizing simultaneously the incestuous dream which motivates his stage fathers and the equivocal nature of his own erotic mythology.

He did not do full justice to the former until the time of *Pericles, Prince of Tyre*, but he exposed the latter quite candidly through Antonio, especially in that courtroom swan song in which the merchant for once nearly becomes a poet.

> I am a tainted wether of the flock,
> Meetest for death. The weakest kind of fruit
> Drops earliest to the ground, and so let me.

Antonio, however, does not die in fact; for this is comedy, and no father may be killed on scene — except symbolically, of course. So Portia's life-denying father is killed a second time to free his daughter from a death in life, and Shylock is killed by conversion-confiscation to be reborn a Christian, baptized like a newborn babe, the holy water canceling out his *brith*, the seal of the covenant in his flesh.

But Shylock is not reborn, dying to Shakespeare forever when he ceases to be "the Jew," as his absence from act 5 reveals. Yet it is not Christianity which kills him, in this play in which no self-styled Christian really goes to church — only Shylock to his synagogue. When Portia, for instance, says at one point that she is betaking herself to a monastery "to live in prayer and contemplation . . . until . . . my lord's return," the "lord" of her equivocal phrase is her lover on earth not her God in heaven; and she is again lying, as in the early casket scenes.

Indeed, she is almost always lying (her most triumphant scene a sustained web of prevarication), when she is not performing character assassination, talking courtly smut, or indulging in empty platitudes. Such platitudes are, indeed, themselves a form of lying, or at least a glossing reality with pieties too familiar to be taken quite as truth. The famous speech on mercy, for instance, delivered in the midst of a scene whose end is vengeance and whose means deceit, is a case in point. Yet critics of Shakespeare, unable to grant the poet a range of irony beyond their own, insist on taking seriously (they fall into the same trap with Polonius on borrowing and lending and with Ulysses on degree) such saccharine banalities as: "It is twice blest;/It blesseth him that gives and him that takes./'Tis mightiest in the mightiest." Nor do they even balk at those silliest lines of all, spoken just before the release of sheer bawdry which ends the play: "How far that little candle throws its beam!/So shines a good deed in a naughty world."

We must not be deceived by what Portia says; neither her morality nor her deepest faith are Christian. What moves her — and what kills Shylock — is hedonism, the pleasure principle. Similarly, what Belmont and gallant Venice alike hold against the Jew is not so much his usury, much less his denial of Christ, but his puritan austerity and his insistence that men are finally *accountable*. When, leaving his house, he turns to warn his daughter:

> What, are there masques? Hear you me, Jessica.
> Lock up my doors, and when you hear the drum
> And the vile squealing of the wry-necked fife,
> Clamber not you up to the casements then,
> Nor thrust your head into the public street
> To gaze on Christian fools with varnished faces,
> But stop my house's ears, I mean my casements.
> Let not the sound of shallow foppery enter
> My sober house.

he is expressing a distaste not just for music and public festival but for the whole code of conspicuous consumption and the ethics it implies. And how could one to whom the Law is all condone a world in which everyone forgives in advance the profligacy of everyone else (of his *own kind*, of course) and no one is held accountable for anything.

But such a code is as incompatible with Roman honor as with Jewish thrift, and so Antonio — whom Bassanio describes as "one in whom/The ancient Roman honor more appears/Than any that draws breath in Italy" — must also go down before it. Being, however, a Roman rather than a Jewish father, he is also a lover rather than a killer; and so he does not confront the pleasure principle head-on in rage, but strives to accommodate to it, compromise with it, even subsidize it with his hard-won capital. In the end, of course, nothing avails. But how he struggles before that end — how Shakespeare struggles for him: that advocate of an austere Uranian love, for whose sake the older lover educates to manliness the boy he adores, and in whose name he is prepared to die, though he knows he cannot ask as much in return, since that boy must rather die to him by marriage. There is not even a proper symbol for his connection with Bassanio in a play in which all other relations are represented by some outward and visible sign. But Antonio attempts to preempt for that purpose the ring, an effort doomed from the start, since the ring, by long tradition, stands for marriage and for female sexuality itself.

Nonetheless, for lack of an alternative, the ring, as the play moves from the fourth into the fifth act, comes to stand for Antonio's efforts to hang on to his "son," as the bond had stood for Shylock's efforts to destroy him and the three caskets had symbolized the mortmain of Portia's father. Giving that ring to Bassanio first, since it is hers to begin with, Portia says: "Myself and what is mine to you and yours/Is now converted. . . . I give them with this ring. . . ." It is an anticipation of the wedding ceremony in which the golden girl and all her golden dowry will be converted from the Golden Fleece into what Gratiano calls "a hoop of gold . . . whose posy was/For all the world like cutler's poetry/Upon a knife, 'Love me, and leave me not.' " But a "hoop" means a restraint; while the word "knife" inevitably evokes the threat of castration. And we are left wondering how the free gift, the longed-for prize, has thus become a fetter, a menace.

The answer is obvious, foreknown. Even in the world of the pleasure principle, love turns to marriage as youth fades toward age; and the marriage contract contains a restriction, a penalty analogous to those written in a dead man's will or a Jew's bond: forsaking all others, *or else*. And how can the free association of Uranian love, bound by no bond, threatening no forfeiture, compete with so exclusive a commitment? For a brief moment, it has seemed possible to Antonio that he and Portia might somehow share his friend ("Mine be thy love's, and thy love's use their treasure"), as, carried away by the pathos of the courtroom scene, Bassanio boasts: "But life itself, my wife, and all the world. . . . I would lose all . . . here to this devil, to deliver you."

This Roman sentiment, however, sets Portia in her disguise to muttering, "Your wife would give you little thanks for that. . . ."; and it prompts Shylock to cry out, as we have earlier remarked, "These be the Christian husbands." For Antonio, it seems more than he had looked for—a happy ending, in fact, after which all else would be anticlimax. Later, therefore, when Portia, playing the lawyer, which is to say, another male, tempts her husband to part with the ring, which, as a woman, she had bade him keep as long as he would keep her love, he is emboldened enough to plead:

> Let his deservings and my love withal
> Be valued 'gainst your wife's commandment.

He puts it wickedly enough: "my love" against her "commandment," affection against mere duty; and it seems to work, bringing him a momentary triumph which Portia does not easily forgive him. Yet it is for him only a delusive victory, since the "boy" who gets the ring is really she, a good witch, who, possessing the only real power in the play (her dream, we know by now, not Antonio's, motivates the plot), gets everything. And there is one more thing which she desires: real revenge for that seeming victory, which in the final sense, she has.

At home again in Belmont, she receives Antonio coolly, even her customary sham of courtesy withheld, until he has, step by step, apologized, recanted, set things right. At first, she quite ignores him, speaking of him in the third person, as if he were not there, while she quibbles with Bassanio on the word "bound": "You should in all sense be much bound to him,/For, as I hear, he has much bound for you." And to this, Antonio, sensing her resentment, answers, "No more than I am acquitted of." It is apparently the right tack, for she bids him welcome at last, though briefly as well as belatedly, then hurls herself into the quarrel about "the ring," already begun by Gratiano and Nerissa: a quarrel which reaches its climax when she and Bassanio swap impassioned speeches, in each of which that obsessive word ends a line five times. "If you did know to whom I gave the ring," is the leitmotif of his; "If you had known the virtue of the ring," of hers.

It is all, of course, pure farce, though only Portia realizes the fact; but it is, for her, farce without a purpose: a burlesque lover's quarrel intended partly as erotic foreplay, partly as a way to even her score with her rival, Antonio. And at last, he rises to the bait, observing in his grave voice, more appropriate for melodrama than burlesque, "I am the unhappy subject of these quarrels," to which she answers, still not quite satisfied, "Sir, grieve not you. You are welcome notwithstanding." And he, who has understood her tenor from the start, does not fail to notice the residual bitterness of that final word, making, during the next interval of their comic bickering, his full recantation.

> I once did lend my body for his wealth,
> Which, but for him that had your husband's ring,
> Had quite miscarried. I dare be bound again,
> My soul upon the forfeit, that your lord
> Will never more break faith advisedly.

It is a speech in which every word counts, though one usually scanted by directors eager to get to the final reconciliations.

"I dare be *bound* again," Antonio says, picking up the word on which Portia had played at the beginning of the scene, and taking us back once more in memory to the original merry bond. Then he continues with "my *soul* upon the forfeit," as if to make quite clear that Portia, like some super-Shylock, will not be contented with a pledge of flesh—out of a sense perhaps that he and Bassanio, eschewing the body, love soul to soul: "my soul upon the forfeit, that your *lord*" — not "*my* love," notice, or "*my* friend," but "your lord/Will never break faith advisedly." This is much, but still, apparently, not enough; for Portia wants the full, the overflowing, measure of revenge. "Then *you* shall be his surety," she insists, forcing him to place the ring once more on his beloved's finger, to give the bridegroom away. "Here, Lord Bassanio," he intones ritually, marrying them, as it were, the second time, "swear to keep this ring." And even to his friend's face now, it is "sweet Bassanio" no longer, but "Lord Bassanio," since, like the long-suffering "I" of the *Sonnets*, he has been taught his place.

There is, however, yet another turn of the screw, as Portia, finally satisfied, grants the defeated Antonio a second semblance of a happy ending. His ships have all come in after all, she assures him, though only she has known until that moment, and he is rich once more. "Sweet lady," he says in his final speech, knowing enough by now not to offend a witch, "you have given me life and living. . . ." And his words seem the very opposite of Shylock's valedictory cry of despair, "You take my life/When you do take the means whereby I live," until we remember that long before, he had told Salarino, ". . . my merchandise makes me not sad." And we suspect it cannot make him joyous either.

In any case, the very last words of the play are not his but Gratiano's, who in their first exchange had spurned Antonio's melancholy, crying, "Let me play the fool." And as the fool, he caps the bawdry to which all four lovers turn after Antonio's recantation and the girls' disclosure of their trick. Cuckoldry is the subject of their jests, since, pretending anger at their husbands' presumed infidelity with the rings, the threat of such betrayal is what had first risen to their minds. Indeed, it seemed thus inevitably to rise to Shakespeare's whenever (as we shall see in *Othello*) he let a comedy run on beyond the marriage that is its natural end. In *Love's Labor's Lost*, in fact, even without the final pairing off, that consequence is projected in a song.

> Cuckoo, cuckoo! Oh, word of fear,
> Unpleasing to a married ear!

In Gratiano's closing couplet, however, not only is the fear of cuckoldry evoked but the final meaning of the ring is revealed, in an allusion to a dirty joke known to almost everyone in Shakespeare's audience and preserved to this very day in a fabliau called "Hans Castorp's Ring." "Well, while I live I'll fear no other thing," Gratiano says, preparing to take his bow, "so sore as keeping safe Nerissa's ring." And the understanders in the pit must have roared with laughter, remembering how in Hans's dream, the Devil slipped a magic ring on his middle finger, promising that so long as he wore it, his wife could never betray him, and how, awaking, Hans found that finger up her cunt.

"To Entrap the Wisest"

René Girard

The criticism of *The Merchant of Venice* has been dominated by two images of Shylock that appear irreconcilable. It is my contention that both images belong to the play and that far from rendering it unintelligible their conjunction is essential to an understanding of Shakespeare's dramatic practice.

The first image is that of the Jewish moneylender in the late-medieval and modern book of anti-Semitism. The mere evocation of that Jewish stereotype suggests a powerful system of binary oppositions that does not have to be fully developed to pervade the entire play. First comes the opposition between Jewish greed and Christian generosity, between revenge and compassion, between the crankiness of old age and the charm of youth, between the dark and the luminous, the beautiful and the ugly, the gentle and the harsh, the musical and the unmusical, and so on.

There is a second image that comes only after the stereotype has been firmly implanted in our minds; at first it does not make as strong an impression as the first, but it gathers strength later on because the language and behavior of the Christian characters repeatedly confirm the rather brief but essential utterances of Shylock himself on which it primarily rests.

The symmetry between the explicit venality of Shylock and the implicit venality of the other Venetians cannot fail to be intended by the playwright. It is true that Bassanio's courtship of Portia is presented primarily as a financial operation. In his plea for Antonio's financial support, Bassanio mentions first the wealth of the young heiress, then her beauty, then finally her spiritual qual-

From *Literature and Society — Selected Papers from The English Institute*, no. 3. © 1980 by The English Institute. The Johns Hopkins University Press, 1980. Originally entitled " 'To Entrap the Wisest': A Reading of *The Merchant of Venice*."

ities. Those critics who idealize the Venetians write as if the many textual clues that contradict their view were not planted by the author himself, as if their presence in the play were a purely fortuitous matter, like the arrival of a bill in the morning mail when one really expects a love letter. On every possible occasion Shakespeare pursued the parallel between the amorous venture of Bassanio and the typical Venetian business of Antonio, his commerce on the high seas. Observe, for instance, the manner in which Gratiano, who is just back from Belmont and still flushed with the success of this expedition, addresses Salerio:

> Your hand, Salerio. What's the news from Venice?
> How doth that royal merchant, good Antonio?
> I know he will be glad of our success.
> We are the Jasons, we have won the fleece.
> SAL. I would you have won the fleece that he hath lost.
>
> (III, ii, 241–46)

The truth is that Bassanio and friends have done exactly that. Even if Antonio's losses turned out to be real, Portia's conquest would more than make up financially for Antonio's ships.

Regarding this symmetry between Shylock and the Venetians, many good points have been made. I will mention only one, for the sole reason that I have not found it in the critical literature on the play. If I am not original, please accept my apologies.

Act 3, scene 2, Bassanio wants to reward his lieutenant for his services, and he tells Gratiano and Nerissa that they will be married simultaneously with Portia and himself, in a double-wedding ceremony — at Portia's expense we may assume. "Our feast," he says, "shall be much honored in your marriage." Upon which the elated Gratiano says to his fiancée: "We'll play with them the first boy for a thousand ducats" (III, ii, 214–17).

These young people have ample reason to be joyous, now that their future is made secure by Bassanio's clever stroke with the caskets, and this bet sounds harmless enough, but Shakespeare is not addicted to pointless social chitchat and must have a purpose. Gratiano's baby will be two thousand ducats cheaper than Antonio's pound of flesh. Human flesh and money in Venice are constantly exchanged for one another. People are turned into objects of financial speculation. Mankind has become a commodity, an exchange value like any other. I cannot believe that Shakespeare did not perceive the analogy between Gratiano's wager and Shylock's pound of flesh.

Shylock's pound of flesh is symbolical of Venetian behavior. The Venetians appear different from Shylock, up to a point. Financial considerations have become so natural to them and they are so embedded into their psyches that they have become not quite but almost invisible; they can never be identified as a distinct aspect of behavior. Antonio's loan to Bassanio, for instance, is treated as an act of love and not as a business transaction.

Shylock hates Antonio for lending money without interest. In his eyes, the merchant spoils the financial business. We can read this as the resentment of vile greed for noble generosity within the context of the first image, but we may prefer another reading that contributes to the second image. The generosity of Antonio may well be a corruption more extreme than the caricatural greed of Shylock. As a rule, when Shylock lends money, he expects more money in return, and nothing else. Capital should produce capital. Shylock does not confuse his financial operations with Christian charity. This is why, unlike the Venetians, he can look like the embodiment of greed.

Venice is a world in which appearances and reality do not match. Of all the pretenders to Portia's hand, Bassanio alone makes the right choice between the three caskets because he alone is a Venetian and knows how deceptive a splendid exterior can be. Unlike his foreign competitors who obviously come from countries where things still are more or less what they seem to be, less advanced countries we might say, he instinctively feels that the priceless treasure he seeks must hide behind the most unlikely appearance.

The symbolic significance of choosing lead rather than the gold and silver selected by the two foreigners faithfully duplicates the whole relationship between the true Venetians and the foreign Shylock. When the two alien pretenders reach avidly for the two precious metals, just like Shylock, they look like personifications of greed; in reality they are rather naive, whereas Bassanio is anything but naive. It is characteristic of the Venetians that they look like the very picture of disinterestedness at the precise moment when their sly calculations cause the pot of gold to fall into their lap.

The generosity of the Venetians is not feigned. Real generosity makes the beneficiary more dependent on his generous friend than a regular loan. In Venice a new form of vassality prevails, grounded no longer in strict territorial borders but in vague financial terms. The lack of precise accounting makes personal indebtedness infinite. This is an art Shylock has not mastered since his own daughter feels perfectly free to rob and abandon him without the slightest remorse. The elegance of the décor and the harmony of the music must not lead us to think that everything is right with the Venetian world. It is impossible, however, to say exactly what is wrong. Antonio is sad but he cannot say why, and this unexplained sadness seems to characterize the whole Venetian business aristocracy as much as Antonio himself.

Even in Shylock's life, however, money and matters of human sentiment finally become confused. But there is something comical in this confusion be-

cause, even as they become one, money and sentiment retain a measure of sepa-
rateness, they remain distinguishable from each other and we hear such things
as "My daughter! Oh, my ducats! Oh, my daughter!/Fled with a Christian!
Oh, my Christian ducats!" (II, viii, 15–16) and other such ridiculous utterances
you would never catch in a Venetian mouth.

There is still another occasion upon which Shylock, goaded by his Venetian
enemies, confuses financial matters with other passions, and it is the affair of
his loan to Antonio. In the interest of his revenge, Shylock demands no interest
for his money, no positive guarantees in case of default, nothing but his infamous
pound of flesh. Behind the mythical weirdness of the request, we have one
spectacular instance of that complete interpenetration between the financial and
the human that is characteristic less of Shylock than of the other Venetians. Thus
Shylock appears most scandalous to the Venetians and to the spectators when
he stops resembling himself to resemble the Venetians even more. The spirit
of revenge drives him to imitate the Venetians more perfectly than before, and,
in his effort to teach Antonio a lesson, Shylock becomes his grotesque double.

Antonio and Shylock are described as rivals of long standing. Of such people
we often say that they have their differences, but this expression would be mis-
leading. Tragic—and comic—conflict amounts to a dissolving of differences that
is paradoxical because it proceeds from the opposite intention. All the people
involved in the process seek to emphasize and maximize their differences. In
Venice, we found, greed and generosity, pride and humility, compassion and
ferocity, money and human flesh, tend to become one and the same. This undifferentiation makes it impossible to define anything with precision, to ascribe
one particular cause to one particular event. Yet on all sides it is the same obsession with displaying and sharpening a difference that is less and less real. Here
is Shylock, for instance, in act 2, scene 5: "Well thou shalt see, thy eyes shall
be thy judges,/The difference between Old Shylock and Bassanio" (II, v, 1–2).
The Christians too are eager to demonstrate that they are different from the
Jews. During the trial scene, it is the turn of the duke, who says to Shylock:
"Thou shalt see the difference of our spirits" (IV, i, 368). Even the words are
the same. Everywhere the same senseless obsession with differences becomes
exacerbated as it keeps defeating itself.

The paradox is not limited to *The Merchant of Venice*. Everywhere in Shakespeare it is an essential component of the tragic and comic relationship. In *The
Comedy of Errors*, the endless efforts of the twins to clear up the confusion created
by that identity between them which they cannot recognize keeps generating
more confusion. The theme of the identical twins, significantly, is borrowed
from Plautus, and it is more than an allegory of the process I am talking about;
it is its mythical transposition. We have an allusion to this process of undifferen-

tiation, I believe, in a well-known line of *The Merchant*. When Portia enters the court she asks, "Which is the merchant and which is the Jew?" (IV, i, 174). Even if she has never met either Antonio or Shylock, we have a right to be surprised Portia cannot identify the Jewish moneylender at first sight, in view of the enormous difference, visible to all, that is supposed to distinguish him from the gracious Venetians. The line would be more striking, of course, if it came after rather than before the following one: "Antonio and old Shylock both stand forth" (IV, i, 175). If Portia were still unable to distinguish Shylock from Antonio once the two men have come forward together, the scene would explicity contradict the primary image of Shylock, the stereotype of the Jewish moneylender. This contradiction would stretch the limits of dramatic credibility beyond the breaking point, and Shakespeare refrained from it, but he went as far as he could, I believe, here and elsewhere, to question the reality of a difference he himself, of course, had first introduced into his play. Even the structure of the line, with its two symmetrical questions, suggests the prevalence of symmetry between the two men. The repetition of the interrogative *which* occurs elsewhere in Shakespeare to suggest the perplexity of observers confronted with items that should be different enough to be clearly differentiated but no longer are. In *A Midsummer Night's Dream*, for instance, the undifferentiation of nature, the confusion of the year's four seasons, precedes and announces the undifferentiation of the four lovers, and the monstrous undifferentiation of Bottom, at the height of the midsummer madness:

> The spring, the summer,
> The childing autumn, angry winter change
> Their wonted liveries, and the mazed world
> By their increase, now knows not which is which.
> (II, i, 111–14)

This analysis must lead to Shylock's famous tirade on reciprocity and revenge; we now have the context in which the meaning and purpose of the passage become unmistakable:

> if you tickle us,
> Do we not laugh? if you poison us, do we not
> Die? and if you wrong us, shall we not revenge?
> If we are like you in the rest, we will resemble
> You in that. If a Jew wrong a Christian, what
> Is his humility? Revenge. If a Christian wrong
> A Jew, what should his sufferance be by Christian
> Example? Why, revenge. The villainy

> You teach me, I will execute; and it shall go
> Hard but I will better the instruction.
>   (III, i, 67–76)

The text insists above all on Shylock's personal commitment to revenge. It does not support the type of "rehabilitation" naively demanded by certain revisionists. But it unequivocally defines the symmetry and the reciprocity that govern the relations between the Christians and Shylock. It says the same thing as the line: "Which is the merchant and which is the Jew?" It is as essential, therefore, as it is striking, and it fully deserves to be singled out.

With his caricatural demand for a pound of flesh, Shylock does, indeed, "better the instruction." What we have just said in the language of psychology can be translated into religious terms. Between Shylock's behavior and his words, the relationship is never ambiguous. His interpretation of the law may be narrow and negative but we can count on him for acting according to it and for speaking according to his actions. In the passage on revenge, he alone speaks a truth that the Christians hypocritically deny. The truth of the play is revenge and retribution. The Christians manage to hide that truth even from themselves. They do not live by the law of charity, but this law is enough of a presence in their language to drive the law of revenge underground, to make this revenge almost invisible. As a result, this revenge becomes more subtle, skillful, and feline than the revenge of Shylock. The Christians will easily destroy Shylock but they will go on living in a world that is sad without knowing why, a world in which even the difference between revenge and charity has been abolished.

Ultimately we do not have to choose between a favorable and an unfavorable image of Shylock. The old critics have concentrated on Shylock as a separate entity, an individual substance that would be merely juxtaposed to other individual substances and remain unaffected by them. The ironic depth in *The Merchant of Venice* results from a tension not between two static images of Shylock, but between those textual features that strengthen and those features that undermine the popular idea of an insurmountable difference between Christian and Jew.

It is not excessive to say that characterization itself, as a real dramatic problem or as a fallacy, is at stake in the play. On the one hand Shylock is portrayed as a highly differentiated villain. On the other hand he tells us himself that there are no villains and no heroes; all men are the same, especially when they are taking revenge on each other. Whatever differences may have existed between them prior to the cycle of revenge are dissolved in the reciprocity of reprisals and retaliation. Where does Shakespeare stand on this issue? Massive evidence from the other plays as well as from *The Merchant* cannot leave the question in doubt. The main object of satire is not Shylock the Jew. But Shylock is rehabilitated only to the extent that the Christians are even worse than he is and that the "honesty" of his vices makes him almost a refreshing figure compared to the sanctimonious ferocity of the other Venetians.

The trial scene clearly reveals how implacable and skillful the Christians can be when they take their revenge. In this most curious performance, Antonio begins as the defendant and Shylock as the plaintiff. At the end of one single meeting the roles are reversed and Shylock is a convicted criminal. The man has done no actual harm to anyone. Without his money, the two marriages, the two happy events in the play, could not have come to pass. As his triumphant enemies return to Belmont loaded with a financial and human booty that includes Shylock's own daughter, they still manage to feel compassionate and gentle by contrast with their wretched opponent.

When we sense the injustice of Shylock's fate, we usually say: Shylock is a scapegoat. This expression, however, is ambiguous. When I say that a character in a play is a scapegoat, my statement can mean two different things. It can mean that this character is unjustly condemned from the perspective of the writer. The conviction of the crowd is presented as irrational by the writer himself. In this first case, we say that in that play there is a theme or motif of the scapegoat.

There is a second meaning to the idea that a character is a scapegoat. It can mean that, from the perspective of the writer, this character is justly condemned, but in the eyes of the critic who makes the statement, the condemnation is unjust. The crowd that condemns the victim is presented as rational by the writer, who really belongs to that crowd; only in the eyes of the critic are the crowd and the writer irrational and unjust.

The scapegoat, this time, is not a theme or motif at all; it is not made explicit by the writer, but if the critic is right in his allegations, there must be a scapegoat effect at the origin of the play, a collective effect probably, in which the writer participates. The critic may think, for instance, that a writer who creates a character like Shylock, patterned after the stereotype of the Jewish moneylender, must do so because he personally shares in the anti-Semitism of the society in which this stereotype is present.

When we say that Shylock is a scapegoat, our statement remains vague and critically useless unless we specify if we mean the scapegoat as theme or the scapegoat as structure, the scapegoat as an object of indignation and satire or the scapegoat as a passively accepted delusion.

Before we can resolve the critical impasse to which I referred at the beginning of my presentation we must reformulate it in the terms of this still unperceived alternative between the scapegoat as structure and the scapegoat as theme. Everyone agrees that Shylock is a scapegoat, but is he the scapegoat of his society only or of Shakespeare's as well?

What the critical revisionists maintain is that the scapegoating of Shylock is not a structuring force but a satirical theme. What the traditionalists maintain is that scapegoating, in *The Merchant of Venice*, is a structuring force rather than a theme. Whether we like it or not, they say, the play shares in the cultural anti-Semitism of the society. We should not allow our literary piety to blind us to the fact.

My own idea is that the scapegoat is both structure and theme in *The Merchant of Venice*, and that the play, in this essential respect at least, is anything any reader wants it to be, not because Shakespeare is as confused as we are when we use the word *scapegoat* without specifying, but for the opposite reason: he is so aware and so conscious of the various demands placed upon him by the cultural diversity of his audience; he is so knowledgeable in regard to the paradoxes of mimetic reactions and group behavior that he can stage a scapegoating of Shylock entirely convincing to those who want to be convinced and simultaneously undermine that process with ironic touches that will reach only those who can be reached. Thus he was able to satisfy the most vulgar as well as the most refined audiences. To those who do not want to challenge the anti-Semitic myth, or Shakespeare's own espousal of that myth, *The Merchant of Venice* will always sound like a confirmation of that myth. To those who do challenge these same beliefs, Shakespeare's own challenge will become perceptible. The play is not unlike a perpetually revolving object that, through some mysterious means, would always present itself to each viewer under aspects best suited to his own perspective.

Why are we reluctant to consider this possibility? Both intellectually and ethically, we assume that scapegoating cannot be and should not be a theme of satire and a structuring force at the same time. Either the author participates in the collective victimage and he cannot see it as unjust or he can see it as unjust and he should not connive in it, even ironically. Most works of art do fall squarely on one side or the other of that particular fence. Rewritten by Arthur Miller, Jean-Paul Sartre or Bertolt Brecht, *The Merchant* would be different indeed. But so would a *Merchant of Venice* that would merely reflect the anti-Semitism of its society, as a comparison with Marlowe's *Jew of Malta* immediately reveals.

If we look carefully at the trial scene, no doubt can remain that Shakespeare undermines the scapegoat effects just as skillfully as he produces them. There is something frightening in this efficiency. This art demands a manipulation and therefore an intelligence of mimetic phenomena that transcends not only the ignorant immorality of those who submit passively to victimage mechanisms but also the moralism that rebels against them but does not perceive the irony generated by the dual role of the author. Shakespeare himself must first generate at the grossly theatrical level the effects that he later undermines at the level of allusions.

Let us see how Shakespeare can move in both directions at the same time. Why is it difficult not to experience a feeling of relief and even jubilation at the discomfiture of Shylock? The main reason, of course, is that Antonio's life is supposed to be under an immediate threat. That threat stems from Shylock's stubborn insistence that he is entitled to his pound of flesh.

Now the pound of flesh is a mythical motif. We found earlier that it is a highly significant allegory of a world where human beings and money are constantly exchanged for one another, but it is nothing more. We can imagine a purely mythical context in which Shylock could really carve up his pound of flesh and Antonio would walk away, humiliated and diminished but alive. In *The Merchant of Venice*, the mythical context is replaced by a realistic one. We are told that Antonio could not undergo this surgical operation without losing his life. It is certainly true in a realistic context, but it is also true, in that same context, that, especially in the presence of the whole Venetian establishment, old Shylock would be unable to perform this same operation. The myth is only partly demythologized, and Shylock is supposed to be capable of carving up Antonio's body in cold blood because, as a Jew and a moneylender, he passes for a man of unusual ferocity. This presumed ferocity justifies our own religious prejudice.

Shakespeare knows that victimage must be unanimous to be effective, and no voice is effectively raised in favor of Shylock. The presence of the silent Magnificoes, the elite of the community, turns the trial into a rite of social unanimity. The only characters not physically present are Shylock's daughter and his servant, and they are of one mind with the actual scapegoaters since they were the first to abandon Shylock after taking his money. Like a genuine Biblical victim, Shylock is betrayed "even by those of his own household."

As scapegoating affects more and more people and tends toward unanimity, the contagion becomes overwhelming. In spite of its judicial and logical nonsense, the trial scene is enormously performative and dramatic. The spectators and readers of the play cannot fail to be affected and cannot refrain from experiencing Shylock's defeat as if it were their own victory. The crowd in the theater becomes one with the crowd on the stage. The contagious effect of scapegoating extends to the audience. In *The Merchant of Venice*, at least, and perhaps in many other plays, the Aristotelian catharsis is a scapegoat effect.

As an embodiment of Venetian justice, the duke should be impartial, but at the very outset of the proceedings he commiserates with the defendant and launches into a diatribe against Shylock:

> I am sorry for thee. Thou art come to answer
> A stony adversary, an inhuman wretch,
> Uncapable of pity, void and empty
> From any dram of mercy.
>
> (IV, i, 3–6)

These words set the tone for the entire scene. The Christian virtue par excellence, mercy is the weapon with which Shylock is clubbed over the head. The Christians use the word *mercy* with such perversity that they can justify their own revenge with it, give full license to their greed and still come out with a clear conscience. They feel they have discharged their obligation to be merciful by their constant repetition of the word itself. The quality of their mercy is not strained, to say the least. It is remarkably casual and easy. When the duke severely asks: "How shalt thou hope for mercy, rendering none?" (IV, i, 88), Shylock responds with impeccable logic: "What judgment shall I dread, doing no wrong?" (IV, i, 89).

Shylock trusts in the law too much. How could the law of Venice be based on mercy, how could it be equated with the golden rule, since it gives the Venetians the right to own slaves and it does not give slaves the right to own Venetians? How can we be certain that Shakespeare, who engineered that scapegoat effect so skillfully, is not fooled by it even for one second? Our certainty is perfect and it may well be much more than "subjective," as some critics would say. It may well be perfectly "objective" in the sense that it correctly recaptures the author's intention and yet it remains a closed book to a certain type of reader. If irony were demonstrable it would cease to be irony. Irony must not be explicit enough to destroy the efficiency of the scapegoat machine in the minds of those fools for whom that machine was set up in the first place. Irony cannot fail to be less tangible than the object on which it bears.

Some will object that my reading is "paradoxical." It may well be, but why should it be a priori excluded that Shakespeare can write a paradoxical play? Especially if the paradox on which the play is built is formulated most explicitly at the center of that very play. Shakespeare is writing, not without a purpose, I suppose, that appearances, especially the appearances of beautiful language, are "The seeming truth which cunning times put on/To entrap the wisest" (III, ii, 100–101). Shakespeare is writing, not without a purpose, that the worst sophistry, when distilled by a charming voice, can decide the outcome of a trial, or that the most unreligious behavior can sound religious if the right words are mentioned. Let us listen to the reasons given by Bassanio for trusting in lead rather than in silver or gold and we will see that they apply word for word to the play itself:

> The world is still deceived with ornament.
> In law, what plea so tainted and corrupt
> But being seasoned with a gracious voice,
> Obscures the show of evil? In religion,
> What damned error but some sober brow
> Will bless it, and approve it with a text,
> Hiding the grossness with fair ornament?
> There is no vice so simple but assumes
> Some mark of virtue on his outward parts.
>
> (III, ii, 74–82)

This is so appropriate to the entire play that it is difficult to believe it a coincidence.

I see Bassanio's brief intervention during the trial scene as another sign of Shakespeare's ironic distance. As soon as Shylock begins to relent, under the pressure of Portia's skill, Bassanio declares his willingness to pay back the money Shylock is now willing to accept. In his eagerness to be finished with the whole unpleasant business, Bassanio shows a degree of mercy, but Portia remains adamant. Feeling her claws in Shylock's flesh, she drives them deeper and deeper in order to exact her own pound of flesh. Bassanio's suggestion bears no fruit but its formulation at this crucial moment cannot be pointless. It is the only reasonable solution to the whole affair but dramatically it cannot prevail because it is undramatic. Shakespeare is too good a playwright not to understand that the only good solution, from a theatrical standpoint, is the scapegoating of Shylock. On the other hand he wants to point out the unjust nature of the "cathartic" resolution that is forced upon him by the necessity of his art. He wants the reasonable solution to be spelled out somewhere inside the play.

Is it not excessive to say that scapegoating is a recognizable motif in *The Merchant of Venice*? There is one explicit allusion to the scapegoat in the play. It occurs at the beginning of Shylock's trial.

> I am a tainted wether of the flock,
> Meetest for death. The weakest kind of fruit
> Drops earliest to the ground, and so let me.
> You cannot better be employed, Bassanio,
> Than to live still and write mine epitaph.
>
> (IV, i, 114–18)

Is there a difficulty for my thesis in the fact that Antonio rather than Shylock utters these lines? Not at all, since their mutual hatred has turned Antonio and Shylock into the doubles of each other. This mutual hatred makes all reconciliation impossible—nothing concrete separates the antagonists, no genuinely tangible issue that could be arbitrated and settled—but the undifferentiation generated by this hatred paves the way for the only type of resolution that can conclude this absolute conflict, the scapegoat resolution.

Antonio speaks these lines in reply to Bassanio, who has just asserted he would never let his friend and benefactor die in his place. He would rather die himself. Neither one will die, of course, or even suffer in the slightest. In the city of Venice, no Antonio or Bassanio will ever suffer as long as there is a Shylock to do the suffering for them.

There is no serious danger that Antonio will die, but he can really see himself, at this point, as a scapegoat in the making. Thus Shakespeare can have an explicit reference to scapegoating without pointing directly to Shylock. There is a great irony, of course, not only in the fact that the metaphor is displaced, the scapegoat being the essence of metaphoric displacement, but also in the almost romantic complacency of Antonio, in his intimation of masochistic satisfaction. The quintessential Venetian, Antonio, the man who is sad without a cause, may be viewed as a figure of the modern subjectivity characterized by a strong propensity toward self-victimization or, more concretely, by a greater and greater interiorization of a scapegoat process that is too well understood to be reenacted as a real event in the real world. Mimetic entanglements cannot be projected with complete success onto all the Shylocks of this world, and the scapegoat process tends to turn back upon itself and become reflective. What we have, as a result, is a masochistic and theatrical self-pity that announces the romantic subjectivity. This is the reason why Antonio is eager to be "sacrificed" in the actual presence of Bassanio.

Irony is not demonstrable, I repeat, and it should not be, otherwise it would disturb the catharsis of those who enjoy the play at the cathartic level only. Irony is anticathartic. Irony is experienced in a flash of complicity with the writer at his most subtle, against the larger and coarser part of the audience that remains blind to these subtleties. Irony is the writer's vicarious revenge against the revenge that he must vicariously perform. If irony were too obvious, if it were intelligible to all, it would defeat its own purpose because there would be no more object for irony to undermine.

The reading I propose can be strengthened, I believe, through a comparison with other plays, notably *Richard III*. When Shakespeare wrote this play, his king's identity as a villain was well established. The dramatist goes along with the popular view, especially at the beginning. In the first scene, Richard presents himself as a monstrous villain. His deformed body is a mirror for the self-confessed ugliness of his soul. Here too we are dealing with a stereotype, the stereotype of the bad king that can be said to be generated or revived by the unanimous rejection of the scapegoat king, the very process that is reenacted in the last act after gathering momentum throughout the play.

If we forget for a while the introduction and the conclusion to focus on the drama itself, a different image of Richard emerges. We are in a world of bloody political struggles. All adult characters in the play have committed at least one political murder or benefited from one. As critics like Murray Krieger and Ian Kott have pointed out, the War of the Roses functions as a system of political rivalry and revenge in which every participant is a tyrant and a victim in turn, always behaving and speaking not according to permanent character differences but to the position he occupies at any moment within the total dynamic system. Being the last coil in that infernal spiral, Richard may kill more people more cynically than his predecessors, but he is not essentially different. In order to make the past history of reciprocal violence dramatically present, Shakespeare resorts to the technique of the curse. Everyone keeps cursing everyone else so vehemently and massively that the total effect is tragic or almost comic according to the mood of the spectator; all these curses mutually cancel each other until the end, when they all converge against Richard and bring about his final undoing, which is also the restoration of peace.

Two images of the same character tend to alternate, one highly differentiated and one undifferentiated. In the case of *The Merchant of Venice* and *Richard III* some fairly obvious reasons can be invoked; in both plays, the theme was a sensitive one, dominated by social and political imperatives regarding which Shakespeare felt skeptical, obviously, but that he could not attack openly. The method he devised permitted an indirect satire, highly effective with the knowledgeable few and completely invisible to the ignorant multitude, avid only of the gross *catharsis* Shakespeare never failed to provide.

Some kind of social and political interpretation is unavoidable, I believe, but it is not incompatible, far from it, with a more radical approach.

Great theater is necessarily a play of differentiation and undifferentiation. The characters will not hold the interest of the audience unless the audience can sympathize with them or deny them its sympathy. They must be highly differentiated, in other words, but any scheme of differentiation is synchronic and static. In order to be good, a play must be dynamic rather than static. The dynamics of the theater are the dynamics of human conflict, the reciprocity of retribution and revenge; the more intense the process, the more symmetry you tend to have, the more everything tends to become the same on both sides of the antagonism.

In order to be good a play must be as reciprocal and undifferentiated as possible but it must be highly differentiated, too, otherwise the spectators will not be interested in the outcome of the conflict. These two requirements are incompatible, but a playwright who cannot satisfy both simultaneously is obviously not a great playwright; he will produce either plays too differentiated which will be labeled *pièces à thèse* because they will be experienced as insufficiently dynamic, or plays too undifferentiated, in order to have a lot of action, or suspense, as we say, but this suspense will appear pointless and will be blamed for a lack of intellectual and ethical content.

The successful playwright can fulfill the two contradictory requirements simultaneously, even though they are contradictory. How does he do it? In many instances he does not seem fully aware of what he is doing; he must do it in the same instinctive manner as the spectators who passionately identify with one antagonist. Even though the assumed difference between the two always translates itself into reciprocal and undifferentiated behavior, our view of the conflict tends to be static and differentiated.

We can be certain, I believe, that such is not the case with Shakespeare. Shakespeare is fully conscious of the gap between the difference of the static structure and the nondifference of tragic action. He fills his plays with ironic allusions to the gap between the two and he does not hesitate to widen that gap still further, as if he knew that he could do this with impunity and that in all probability he would be rewarded for doing it; far from destroying his credibility as a creator of "characters" he would increase the overall dramatic impact of his theater and turn his plays into those dynamic and inexhaustible objects upon which critics can comment endlessly without ever putting their finger on the real source of their ambiguity.

In *Richard III* we have examples of this practice no less striking than in *The Merchant of Venice*. Anne and Elizabeth, the two women who have most suffered at the hands of Richard, cannot resist the temptation of power, even at the cost of an alliance with him, when Richard himself diabolically dangles this toy in front of them. After cursing Richard abundantly and discharging in this manner all her moral obligations, Anne literally walks over the dead body of her father to join hands with Richard. A little later Elizabeth walks over the dead bodies of two of her children, symbolically at least, in order to deliver a third one into the bloody hands of the murderer.

These two scenes are structurally close, and they generate a crescendo of abomination that cannot be without a purpose. These two women are even more vile than Richard, and the only character who is able to point out this vileness, thus becoming in a sense the only ethical voice in the whole play, is Richard himself, whose role, *mutatis mutandis*, is comparable to that of Shylock in *The Merchant of Venice*.

It is Shakespeare's genius that he can do such things. And he does them, not to generate irony only, but for the sake of dramatic efficiency. He knows that by doing them, he creates uneasiness among the spectators, he places upon them a moral burden with which they cannot deal in terms of the scapegoat values presented at the outset. The demand for the expulsion of the scapegoat is paradoxically reinforced by the very factors that make this expulsion arbitrary.

I fully agree that, in the case of plays like *Richard III* or *The Merchant of Venice*, an infinite number of readings is possible, and this infinity is determined by "the play of the signifier." I do not agree that this play is gratuitous, and that it is in the nature of all signifiers as signifiers to produce such infinite play. The literary signifier always becomes a victim. It is a victim of the signified, at least metaphorically, in the sense that its play, its *différence*, or what you will, is almost inevitably sacrificed to the one-sidedness of a single-minded differentiated structure à la Lévi-Strauss. The sacrificed signifier disappears behind the signified. Is this victimage of the signifier nothing but a metaphor, or is it mysteriously connected to the scapegoat as such in the sense that it is rooted in that ritual space where the major signifier is also a victim, not merely in the semiotic sense, this time, but in the sense of Shylock or of Richard III? The play of the signifier, with its arbitrary interruption for the sake of a differentiated structure, operates exactly like the theatrical and ritual process, with its conflictual undifferentiation suddenly resolved and returned to static differentiation through the elimination of a victim. Everything I have said suggests that to Shakespeare, at least, all these things are one and the same. The process of signification is one with the scapegoat resolution of the crisis in which all significations are dissolved, then reborn—the crisis that is described at length in *Troilus and Cressida* and designated as the "crisis of Degree." The evidence from ritual as well as from mythology suggests that Shakespeare may well be right. Long before *deciders* acquired its more abstract significance—to decide—it meant to cut with a knife, to immolate a sacrificial victim.

Those who think that the problem of textuality can be disposed of with no regard for the victims to which literary texts allude should have a close look at *The Merchant of Venice*.

The Wether and the Ewe: Verbal Usury

Marc Shell

Soon after the vernacular grail tales first appeared in Europe, new financial institutions began to challenge the theories of production and representation by which the tales were informed. Fiduciary means disturbingly similar to the Christian cornucopia that is the grail affected more and more the livelihood and thinking of impoverished aristocrats and merchants. The *topos* of the *roi-pecheur* (sinner/fisher-king) was displaced by the Venetian "merchant prince." This "royal merchant," both landed aristocrat and monied trader, sought the golden fleece with marine fleets supported by interest loans and insurance. The divine store generated gratis from the holy grail was replaced conceptually by the natural store of alien shores whose wealth had to be husbanded or exploited by expensive means. The problems of divine economy and of the difference between producer and product came to be considered in terms of nature and the tension between natural and unnatural representation and exchange.

Generation or production is the principal topic of Shakespeare's *The Merchant of Venice*. In this play the quest for material and spiritual riches — for money and love — involves two related conceptual difficulties: the similarity between natural sexual generation and monetary generation, and the apparent commensurability (even identity) of men and money. The revelation of these difficulties depends for its dramatic expression on a series of bonds in which individuals and properties are exchanged for each other. The play generates a grand political and economic critique of human production that, in a few hours, runs through the whole gamut of familial and political associations.

From *The Kenyon Review* 1, no. 4 (Fall 1979). © 1979 by Kenyon College. Originally entitled "The Wether and the Ewe: Verbal Usury in *The Merchant of Venice*."

Use, Ewes, and Iewes

Antonio is an unfortunate "royal merchant" whose purse is exhausted and whose personal part in this comedy is sad. This *roi-pecheur* claims that neither money nor love saddens him. Yet the only person he loves, Bassanio, owes him "in money and in love" (I.i.131) and is "plot[ting] to get clear of all the debts [he] owes." Bassanio would free himself from Antonio, whose present lack of funds diminishes Bassanio's once "noble rate" of living. He would attach himself to one more "worthy" than Antonio. Antonio offers to aid Bassanio with "[his] purse, [his] person" (138–39) but, as Bassanio already knows, these are insufficient. All that Antonio can do is borrow a purse for his friend by hazarding a vital part of his person.

Need to supplement oneself or one's own leads thus to borrowing and to tension between two ideas about moneylending. The first idea (that of the Greeks) focuses on breeding and the relationship of monetary generation to animal generation. The second idea (that of the Hebrews) focuses on the classification of groups of human beings and the laws concerning bonds that divide and join them together. These ideas are elucidated in the interview between Antonio, who says that his custom is neither to give nor to take unfair "advantage" or "excess," and Shylock, whose means of livelihood is usury.

"Few [persons]," writes Francis Bacon, "have spoken usefully of usury." Shakespeare's Shylock is one of them. Shylock is not a miser of words (which is what Mark Van Doren calls him) but rather (as Sigurd Burckhardt suggests) a user of words. To my knowledge, no one since the medieval era has devoted attention to the category of verbal usury in jurisprudence, rhetoric, and philosophy. (The phrase "verbal usury" has been consistently overlooked even by compilers of dictionaries.) Yet "verbal usury" is an important technical term in the Jewish Talmud, in the Christian church fathers, and in the Islamic Traditions. There it refers to the generation of an illegal — the church fathers say unnatural — supplement of verbal meaning by use of methods such as punning and flattering.

Shylock uses Antonio's words "I do never use it" (I.iii.66) to generate by a pun an argument that would enlarge any debate about "use" to include consideration of the human genealogy of "Iewes" (as Shakespeare spelled "Jews") and also the animal generation of "ewes." Thus he supplements the principal meaning of "use." The genealogy, as we shall see, defines divisions between the Jewish and other peoples, and the generation of ewes serves to locate monetary generation in relation to animal generation. As the Jew uses moneys (which Bacon calls "[the tokens current and accepted] for values") to supplement principals, so he uses puns to exceed the principle meanings of words (which Bacon calls "the tokens current and accepted for conceits").

Shylock argues that, as Jacob's management of the sexual generation of lambs by Laban's "ewes" is natural, so too is the generation of "use" by money. He compares "[sexual] generation" with monetary generation or usury. "Ewes" and "rams," he implies, are like monetary principals, and "lambs" are like monetary "interest" or "use" (I.iii.75–86). Antonio tries to argue against Shylock's position by suggesting that "gold and silver" differ from "ewes and rams" (91). Yet Shylock did not argue that metals are generative (as did many alchemists) but rather that, as Saint Bernardino of Siena says, "money as capital has a creative power (*quandam seminalem rationem*)." Antonio thus misses the point of the Jew's analogy. Antonio does not use even the traditional Aristotelian and Thomist argument against the analogy between reproduction and monetary use: he does not argue that, as Francis Bacon ironically puts it, "it is against nature for money to beget money," or, as Luther says, that "money is the sterile thing." Shylock wants to discuss usury in these Greek and Christian terms, but he is thwarted because Antonio can not or will not recognize any difference between a gold or silver coin and any other kind of piece of gold or silver.

Antonio says that he wants Shylock to lend him money not according to "nature" but rather according to Jewish law:

> lend it not
> As to thy friends—for when did friendship take
> A breed of barren metal of his friend?
>
> (I.iii.128–30)

Antonio refers to the Jewish legal distinction between lending to a "brother" or fellow Jew and lending to an "other." If Antonio were a Jew, suggests Antonio, Shylock would lend money to him gratis. (Tubal will lend money gratis to Shylock who, like Antonio, does not himself have sufficient funds for Bassanio.) Antonio does not seem to understand that this Jewish distinction between brother and other is essentially connected with the problem of natural generation about which he insists that Shylock be silent. He does not see that the only way to determine who is a brother and who is an other is to determine the generation of every one. Such a determination was the aim of Shylock's interrupted genealogy of the Jews which prefaced his tale about the generation of ewes. It was meant to distinguish between Jews and non-Jews.

> When Jacob graz'd his uncle Laban's sheep—
> This Jacob from our holy Abram was,
> As his wise mother wrought in his behalf,
> The third possessor; ay, he was the third—
>
> (I.iii.67–70)

Abraham fathered Isaac who fathered Jacob. Jews suppose that they are the descendants of Jacob. (Shylock often confuses himself with his forefather Jacob. The folio reads "I, he was the third—"; and Jacob's first wife, Leah, was the namesake of Shylock's late wife. Leah was the sister of Rachel, for whose hand in marriage Jacob husbanded Laban's ewes). The argument is complicated by the fact that the two successions—through Isaac and Jacob—to which Shylock refers were challenged. Ishmael, Isaac's older half-brother by Abraham and Hagar, was, according to some, robbed of his birthright. Muslims—the Prince of Morocco, the Turks, the Moorish woman pregnant by Launcelot, and Launcelot, who is "Hagar's offspring" (II.v.42)—suppose that they are the descendants of Ishmael. Esau, by a similar argument, was robbed of his birthright by Jacob, his younger twin brother, who tricked him with a bit of clever merchantry. He exchanged food, which sustains an individual's life, for the possession of the lifeline of the Jewish tribe.

Thus Shylock's discussion in terms of monetary use of the clever Jew's management of the sexual generation of ewes (his forefathers were shepherds as his brothers are moneylenders) is essentially connected with his discussion of the sexual generation of Iewes themselves. By speaking of the generation of Jews Shylock is distinguishing precisely between others and brothers. Antonio fails to see the relationship between breeding and both the divisions of animals into species and the divisions of the human species into linguistic, racial, religious, and other kinds of groups.

For a Christian such as we suppose Antonio to be, a brother is supposed to be any descendant of Adam and not, as for a Jew, a descendant of Jacob. For a Christian there is no need to know a man's individual genealogy to determine if he is a brother. Yet the customs and the laws of the white, Christian Venetians and the practice of Belmont discriminate against others in more extreme ways than does Shylock's distinction between human brothers and others who are human. Shylock does treat Antonio as if he were from an other group of human beings than his own Jewish one, but Antonio treats Shylock as if he were from another species of animal than the human one (a dog). Not to be a Jewish brother is to be less alien to a Jew than not to be a brother is to a Christian. Does Antonio treat Shylock as an animal because he believes that Shylock has some characteristics of the canine or of the "ewe-ish" species or that he lacks some characteristics of the human species? Or is it because Antonio conflates special with tribal characteristics, and so believes that the difference between a human being and another animal is identical to the difference between a member of one's own tribe (a racial, religious, or familial group) and a member of an other tribe? If the latter, then Antonio has transformed the Jewish distinction between human brothers (members of the Jewish tribe) from whom one can not take interest and human strangers (members of any other tribe) from whom one can take interest. He has changed it to a distinction between those beings whose religion is Christianity (a tribe that proselytizes and is theoretically "universal" or at least "humanist") and those whose religions are other than Christianity (in our play Judaism and Islam), and who are, on that account, nonhuman, though convertible to Christianity and human being. Antonio may be one of those people who, if he should say "All men are my brothers," may well mean "Only my brothers are men, all others are animals" or even "Citizens of Italian states (Venice and Belmont) are human, but citizens of other states (Morocco, Turkey, and, if there were such a place, Jewdom) are animals."

If Shylock should wish to lend money to Antonio as if Antonio were a brother to all Jews (descended from Jacob) or as if Shylock were a Christian brother to all men (descended from Adam) he would lend Antonio money without interest, but he might well exact, as Bacon reminds us that good Christians did, a monetary or corporeal penalty if the loan were not paid on time. [A pecuniary penalty was usually not considered interest because it was due only if the debt was not paid on time. Antonio would have done better to pay interest (in the Jewish manner) rather than to forfeit a pound of flesh (in an extreme version of the Christian manner).] Perhaps a monetary penalty would be condemned as an unnatural offspring by a zealot like Antonio who seems to condemn even marine insurance. (It is odd that Antonio does not insure his ships: marine insurance was common in Venice by the fifteenth century and in England by the sixteenth. Perhaps his stated policy against lending or borrowing for profit extends to the institution of insurance, which some thinkers connect conceptually and historically with monetary interest.) Only by taking no interest and substituting a corporeal penalty, then, could Shylock be or appear to be brotherly (gentile) to Antonio. This is what he does. To buy Antonio's friendship Shylock extends this kindness (I.iii.164): he will lend him money and "take no doit/of usance" (136–37). He who spoke of the sexual "deed of kind" between animals (81) says that he would lend Antonio money as though he were a kind kinsman to him (138–39). Adapting the Christian method of securing loans, Shylock announces that he will take as a conditional surety an obligation to pay a corporeal penalty, a pound of flesh. The merchant Antonio, who assured his friend of funds, is very sure of the safe return of his uninsured commercial ventures, and Shylock allays the Christians' fears of danger by insisting that to a Jew "a pound of man's flesh taken from a man is not so estimable, profitable neither,/As flesh of muttons, beefs or goats" (161–63). The flesh of ewes is worth more (to one who is not a human cannibal or a man-eating dog) than flesh of man. By the terms of the contract, then, Shylock substitutes, for the use he would usually take, a conditional security on something supposedly worth less than even ewe's flesh.

Antonio would not speak of use—ewes and Iewes. But the discussion of usury and sexual generation which Antonio would not pursue is soon enacted in the related terms of a series of exchanges of a purse (three-thousand ducats) for a part of a person (a pound of flesh) or for a whole person (since the part may be vital). The apparent commensurability between persons and purses which this enactment reveals turns out to be more typical of Christian law, which allows human beings to be purchased for money, than Jewish "iustice" and practice, which disallow it.

From Courtship to Court

The suitors to the person and purse of Portia believe that the trial by caskets is a hazardous gamble like most commercial ventures and loans. The inscriptions on the caskets would seem to support their opinion. Portia's father, however, established the trial to discover a real man for Portia, or at least a suitable one. The inner mettle of the suitors is supposed to be tested by how well each suitor surmises from the outsides of the three metallically different caskets what the insides contain. Metals—including the silver and gold ones that Antonio said were useless—are supposed to have the useful role of distinguishing the right man for Portia to marry.

Most of Portia's suitors are said to be unmanly and all are threatened with being unmanned. They are unmanly in that they are, in Portia's language, mere "beasts." Portia disqualifies them from Mankind on the basis of outward characteristics such as type of clothing and complexion. She does not consider inward characteristics as measures of Man or of the men who court her: "If [the Prince of Morocco] have the condition of a saint and the complexion of a devil [black], I had rather he should shrive me than wive me" (I.ii.120–22). Her tendency to banish persons from the human species or from the male sex is checked only in jest: "God made [Monsieur Le Bon, who is "every man in no man"], and therefore let him pass for a man" (52–53). Yet we know that being divinely created does not mean that an animal is a man. God made females as well as males and animals as well as humans. Only knowledge of an animal's ontogeny and of its species' phylogeny can determine whether it is a man, horse, monkey, dog, ewe, or something else. Shylock claims to have access to such knowledge: for him, men are the animals descended from Adam ("Adam" means Man) and Jews are the men descended from Jacob.

Among the characteristics Portia heeds is language. Language is both a bond and a barrier between men. The ability to speak is a characteristic that binds men together into a species, but men speak different languages. Men who speak only one language are bound together by their language, but they are barred from speaking with men who speak any other. Because Portia has hardly "a poor pennyworth in the English" and her English suitor "hath neither Latin, French nor Italian" (64–74), for example, the Englishman is to her only a counterfeit of a man: "He is a proper man's picture, but alas! who can converse with a dumb-show?" (66–68). The ability to speak language may distinguish men from the (other) animals, but inability to speak a particular language may make one man as dumb to another man as to any other animal.

The suitors that are, to Portia, not even men, are threatened with being legitimately unmanned. Should a suitor choose the wrong casket he must promise never to generate within the bonds of wedlock his own flesh and blood (II.i.41–42). He will be made as barren as Antonio believes metal to be. His legitimate genealogical bloodline (if not the flesh and blood of his own body) will be cut. He will become, in this legal sense, a castrate.

A black man, outside of whom flows a white robe, is the first to choose. The Prince of Morocco seeks the picture of Portia inside one of the caskets. He must tell the substance from the superficies.

The outside of each casket is like that of a coin and also like that of an inscribed ring: all these items are composed of metal and of an inscription impressed into it. We have seen that failure to distinguish between coins (ducats) and the metals of which they are only partially composed (gold and silver) was associated with Antonio's dangerously hasty dismissal of Shylock's words about monetary generation. Here the "golden mind" (II.vii.20) of Morocco considers each inscribed metal object before him in terms both of its inscription and its metal. He chooses "the saying graved in gold" (36) and, on the basis of a numismatic analogy that confuses the impressed type on a coin—an angel—with what he hopes to find inside the casket—an "angel"—he chooses gold (55–59). The skull that he finds in the engraved gold casket comes from the grave. Morocco thus learns, from the written scroll that accompanies this "carrion Death," that he must now be as barren, legally speaking, as Antonio argued that gold was.

In this context what is striking about the next suitor's method of choosing is that he considers each casket only in terms of its inscription. Arragon "assume[s] desert" (II.ix.50) by coining himself with "the stamp of merit" (38) but without considering the metal of which the coin-like silver is made. Arragon is "sped," yet he is allowed to "take what wife [he] will to bed" (69). Unlike the black Muslim, the white Christian is allowed to try to generate kin in wedlock.

The third trial is that of Bassanio, he in whom the outside appearance and inside reality are most unlike. He uses words, clothing, and gifts to dress up his suit. Portia, who judges men by their glister or lackluster, has chosen for herself this being with a white complexion and with a desire for glistering gold, but she fears that the seeker of gold and silver may choose a casket made of one of the metals he seeks. Though bound to her father's will (which curbs her will) and to the properties that it promises, she planned nevertheless to mislead the young German (I.ii.87–91) and now educates Bassanio to choose the lead casket.

To help Bassanio, Portia orders music to be played. This will have the effect of seasoning Bassanio into becoming more royal and less merchant-like, more like

> young Alcides, when he did redeem
> The virgin tribute paid by howling Troy
> To the sea monster.
> (III.ii.55–57; compare with II.i.32–35)

Then follows a suggestive song about the generation ("breeding," "begetting," "engendering") of fancy, whose first lines end with words that rhyme with "lead" and whose last line "ring[s] fancy's knell" (III.ii.63–70). Bassanio, who still uses fanciful speech and dress, now learns to say that, or act as though, he dismisses them.

> So may the outward shows be least themselves;
> The world is still deceived with ornament.
> In law, what plea so tainted and corrupt
> But being seasoned with a gracious voice,
> Obscures the show of evil?
> (III.ii.73–77)

Bassanio thus criticizes deceivers who use ornament to their evil purpose, perhaps as Antonio believed that Shylock used scriptures. Bassanio does not seem to consider how he himself uses and has used words and gold to purchase "valor's excrement" (87). Nor does he consider that a seasoned voice may generate good as well as bad shows. Portia's song, for example, "seasoned" (V.i.107–8) him to choose the lead casket in the courtship trial, and Balthasar-Portia's voice will obscure Shylock's case in the courtroom trial.

Bassanio, like the losing suitors, considers the problems of exchange about which the inscriptions on the caskets are written. Unlike them, however, he does not consider the inscriptions themselves. He pays heed, significantly, only to the metals (which is what Antonio did when he failed to distinguish between coin and precious metal). Bassanio calls gold a "hard food for Midas" (III.ii.102)—who turned his daughter into gold—and silver a "pale and common drudge/ 'Tween man and man" (103–4). As Karl Marx reminds us, silver is money, the intermediating "drudge" that pays Launcelot and that Bassanio has borrowed to finance his courtship, and it is an ostentatious ornament like the silvery and beguiling tongue of "eloquence" (III.ii.106).

Inside the lead casket he chooses, Bassanio finds the portrait of Portia. But as he has learned to claim cunningly to set aside the "seeming truth which cunning puts on/To entrap the wisest" (100–101), so he knows not to be trapped into confusing this mere "counterfeit" of Portia with the genuinely valuable thing itself. He would win the wealthy "lady of substance," and so presents Portia with his "title" to her: "I come by note" — he means the portrait — "to give and to receive" (139–40). The "note" is a kind of ticket to the person and purse of Portia that Bassanio, as master of etiquette, would "confirm, sign and ratify" with a kiss.

Portia promises Bassanio the "full sum of me" (157). She is a "fulsome ewe" (I.iii.82). Despite all the talk about lead, Portia is not bred so "dull" as lead (III.ii.162). Like gold and silver ducats as the Iewe Shylock interprets them, she can generate riches.

But a fertile ewe, unlike a monetary principal, needs a potent ram to generate offspring. Herein lies an essential connection between the two major plots of the play. The marriage formula must be reciprocal. Bassanio can not reciprocate, can not give, because he is not his own man. Bassanio is about to win the ewe's "golden fleece," (241, compare with I.i.170), but Antonio's marine fleets, his means of livelihood, that were to return gold for the Jew, are lost, and so too may be his life. The danger to Antonio — and the "paper" in which Antonio, who would not use money, encourages Bassanio to "use [his] pleasure" (320) — compels Bassanio to admit that his courtship strategy depended not only on the gentleman's blood that circulates in his veins but also on Antonio's bond and the Jewish money that circulated to him. He is compelled to reveal to Portia that he is already engaged:

> When I told you
> My state was nothing, I should then have told you
> That I was worse than nothing; for indeed
> I have engaged myself to a dear friend,
> Engaged my friend to his mere enemy
> To feed my means
>
> (258–63)

Thus Portia learns that Bassanio did not "give and hazard all he has" (as the inscription on the lead casket, so far ignored by the couple, demanded). He hazarded only the purse of Shylock and the person of Antonio. Antonio, rather than Portia, is his "dearest friend" (292). Portia wanted to marry Bassanio right away (303), as her father required (II.ix.5–6), but now she may fear that her interference in the trial by caskets resulted in her getting a suitor who is (as yet) unsuitable. She encourages him to leave before they marry (III.ii.322).

The commercial fate and love of Antonio have thus "interposed" between

Portia and Bassanio. The problem of monetary "excess" (I.iii.58) that Shylock and Antonio discussed in the bond scene has become the problem of "excess" or "surfeit" in the love between Bassanio and Portia (III.ii.112–14, 157). The courtship cannot be completed until the bond between Shylock and Antonio that made the courtship possible is nullified in court, until Bassanio's engagement to Antonio is somehow voided. The marriage bond cannot be concluded until the commerical bond is cancelled. In the process of its cancellation the nature of the marriage bond and of human bondage in general will be relentlessly explored. . . .

REDEMPTION

The dilemmas involved in the merchant's bond and in the marriage bond are partly exposed when Nerissa pretends to discover that the ring that she, like Portia, gave to her fiancé as a symbolic earnest of their marriage precontract, is missing. Were Balthasar, the *deus ex machina* in the court, and Portia, the *dea in machina* in the courtship, not the same person, the tension in the play would be unresolvable. The transformations of the two Christian women disguised as men at the legal bar back into women are thus necessary to the success of the marriage union, just as was the transformation of the Jewess disguised as a bird-man at the "festive bar" into a woman (Jessica). Woman's manhood is thus essential in this play, but it is also troubling in the context of problems about usury, sexual generation, and the classification of animals into species and subspecies. For example, it is sometimes ambiguous whether women, who do not plead *in propria persona* in court or in courtship, are, like monkeys, members of another species than Man; or whether they are, like *castrati*, deformed or different — perhaps even better — members of the species of Man who are not only brotherly (as descendants of Adam) but also otherly (since they are different from males). The Jew Shylock, the black Morocco, and other aliens are already castrated one way or another, and now Gratiano seems to intuit that the solution to the dilemmas facing them all is connected with castrating the men to whom they gave their rings: "In faith I gave [the ring] to the judge's clerk./Would he were gelt that had it, for my part,/Since you do take it, love, so much at heart" (V.i.143–45). He would unman the man whom we know to have been a woman.

The process of the last scene in *The Merchant of Venice* will indeed "mar the young clerk's pen" (237) by revealing the Clerk (with a penis) to have been Nerissa, whose ring Gratiano, threatened with being cuckolded, finally learns that he must keep safe (306–7).

At this point, however, Gratiano tries to defend his giving the ring to the Clerk by arguing that the ring was a mere "trifle." He claims that it was only

> a hoop of gold, a paltry ring
> That she did give me, whose posy [inscription] was
> For all the world like cutler's poetry
> Upon a knife—'Love me, and leave me not.'
> (V.i.147–50)

The offended Nerissa's rejoinder is that neither the epigrammatic posy inscribed in a ring nor the metal of which the ring is made tells its true value. As in the episodes involving the suitors' interpretations of the inscribed caskets and coins, the gist is that one should attend to more than the statements impressed in and the exchange values of metals. The symptomatic derogation of Nerissa's gold ring by Gratiano further diminishes our trust in the ability of metals to test human metal and in Bassanio's choice of the lead casket. Will Bassanio, who gave Portia's ring to Balthasar, be able to pick up courting Portia where he left off?

Portia agrees to forgive Bassanio for "break[ing] an oath" (248) if he swears the only "oath of credit" she will accept, an oath "by [his] double self" (245). As it happens, Antonio offers to "second" Bassanio. In a striking spiritual recapitulation of the original bond between Antonio and Shylock, which seems to lift that bond from the level of bodies to that of souls, he says:

> I once did lend my body for his wealth,
> Which but for him that had your husband's ring
> Had quite miscarried. I dare be bound again
> My soul upon the forfeit, that your lord
> Will never more break faith advisedly.
> (249–53)

If Antonio at the beginning of the play was a spiritual usurer who lent his body, he becomes at the end a user of money who lends his soul.

In exchange for Antonio's soul as "surety" (254) in this new bargain, Portia gives the ring to Antonio. Antonio, who staked the beginning of the Bassanio-Portia courtship, now oversees its completion when he gives the ring to Bassanio. He marries no woman (he does marry in one of Shakespeare's sources), but he is the one who marries or presides over the union of Portia with Bassanio. Thus the tainted wether plays the role of holy hermit (32). The difficult fix is again "redeemed" by Antonio's personal surety.

Finally the problem of scarcity that drives men to hazardous and saddening ventures is solved by an abundant dispensation. Bassanio seemed to bring to Belmont from Venice a "horn full of good news" (47). His new servant Launcelot even imitates the sound of the post horn (39–44). However, the real cornucopia in *The Merchant of Venice* is the "fulsome ewe" Portia, whose "full sum" displaces or seems to displace the partial sums of the Jews (Shylock and Tubal) and is associable with the quality of mercy that drops gratis from heaven. (Bassanio and Gratiano only *have* horns, as rams and as the cuckholds that Portia and Nerissa jestingly make them out to be.)

Portia manages two dispensations. She gives Antonio the news that his ships are "richly come to harbour" (277). (That Portia knew the contents of the sealed letter that brings this information suggests that these riches may come from her. "You shall not know" says she, "by what strange accident/I chanced on this letter.") And Portia's servant announces that for Lorenzo and Jessica there will be plenty of "manna" (294) — not the food that drops as the gentle dew from heaven but rather the money that Shylock was strained to promise them in his "special deed of gift" (292). Thus the Jew, whose conditional dispensation of wealth to the Christian Antonio was the means by which the courtship of persons in *The Merchant of Venice* began, is connected even with this last apportionment of funds by Portia.

If the kind of generation for which Portia stands is to displace fully that represented by Shylock it must include not only the dispensation or generation of money but also that of natural offspring. Significantly, however, Portia and Bassanio do not themselves mention children. And any hint of natural offspring to be generated by the Christians connects it, as Shylock would and as Antonio would not, with interest or with miscegenation — miscegenation like the generation of an illegitimate child by Launcelot and the black Moorish woman (III.v.35), and like that of the spotted lambs that Shylock compared with interest (I.iii.72–86). For example, a connection with interest is made when Gratiano (Bassanio's foil) looks forward to "couching with the doctor's clerk" (V.i.305). A birth consequent from this act would produce not only a human offspring but also a monetary offspring from Gratiano's and Nerissa's proposed wager with Bassanio and Portia:

> GRATIANO. We'll play with them [Bassanio and Portia] the
>   first boy for a thousand ducats.
> NERISSA. What, and stake down?
> GRATIANO. No, we shall ne'er win at that sport, and stake
>   down.
>
> (III.ii.213–17)

The "stake" is the monetary deposit of the wager, a kind of monetary principal (the instrument used by the investor to generate monetary offspring), and it is also the penis (the instrument of the male progenitor of human offspring). The domestic economy that Portia, champion of marriage, seems to represent, is one in which children (if they exist) will continue to be connected with ducats.

That Shylock's puse and his theory of purses are still behind or substantiate the action of the persons in the last scene is a sign that Belmont, though a place (literally, *topos*) of marriage and abundance, is inextricably linked with commercial exchanges and scarcity. The path from Shylock's doctrine of "life for life" to the corresponding doctrine of Portia suggests that the end of the play does not transcend or fully overcome the dilemmas that gave rise to the action in the beginning.

The *Merchant of Venice* begins in a sad commercial republic and ends in a happier place. It may seem therefore that Venice stands in the same relation to Belmont as a commercial contract to a marriage contract, a torch or candle to a moon, or the music of the earth to the heavenly music of the spheres. It may be that Belmont is "a substitute" that "shines brightly as a king," but it does so only "until a king be by" (V.i.94–95). And what if the king is not there? The apparent contradictions in the end of the play reinforce our impression of the absence of real royalty. The final dispensation only *seems* to lift the ventures of the Venetians' quest for love and money from the level of a human body (Antonio staked his in Venice) to the level of a human soul (Antonio staked his in Belmont) or from merchantry to mercy. The action has demonstrated that souls are as interconnected with bodies as lives (persons) are connected with means of livelihood (purses). The beautiful marriage bond is not far removed from the ugly bond that made it possible in the first place.

Thus topical Belmont is not an Idea like that in Platonic dialectic. The play is generated as Platonic dialectic is, and it divides or classifies the whole of generation into parts as Platonic dialectic does, but the series of contractual hypotheses that generate the dramatic movement of this political play do not cartwheel to the heavens as does Platonic dialectic. That it does not do so lends the play its brilliantly critical aspect.

The *Merchant of Venice* may be treated as a medieval duel (a kind of moot court of law, torture, or combat) in which the synthesis of the dual theses (the defense and the prosecution) is merely an illusion. Perhaps Shylock's early elimination from the stage tends to make us believe or want to believe in the dissolution of the "differences" between Jew and Christian or between moneylender and nobleman. But the drama is not a tragedy in which, as the dialectician Hegel puts it, two opposite forces are cancelled (*aufgehoben*)—destroyed, incorporated, and transcended. (The marriage bond is very like the revenge bond. Since the former is not cancelled—it is rather the expected end—neither can the latter be cancelled anywhere but in Portia's topical court and courtship.) The confrontation between Christian and Jew—"the difference of [their] spirit[s]" (IV.i.366)—or between capitalist merchant and feudal royal aristocrat, and the subsequent conversions between the two groups (Shylock's to Christianity, for example, and the royal-merchant Antonio's to Jewish usury) hints that such a dramatic movement is possible. But the end of the comedy does not depict the tragic destruction of an old order (one that would sweep Venice away) or the creation of a new domestic and political economy. No single bond is genuinely cancelled and redeemed. The fate of Shylock, who sold his revenge, is not a dispensation or reckoning (*moira*) like that parceled out by Greek tragedy but rather an apportionment to him by the comedist Portia.

Yet there are in this comedy suggestions of a tragedy to come. The marriage in Belmont seems to be a stopgap measure taken against the tendency for the dilemmatic relationship between purse and person, which thoroughly informs and drives all aspects of life in Venice, to work itself out by changing the commercial republic from what it is or by destroying it. The marrying Christians elucidate this tendency. They have already begun to shear the golden fleece from the sheep. Should this fleece, like uninsured marine fleets, prove to be less fruitful of spiritual and material wealth than the infinitely generative Holy Grail, they will eventually have again to seek out the money of Tubal. (Tubal was the ultimate source of the three-thousand ducats and he is left almost untouched by the trials of the play.) The Jewish moneylender behind the scenes of the last act of the courtly world is not easily forgotten. The aristocratic court of the comedist Portia cannot long exist without a day of reckoning in the court of tragedy.

The Mind at Ocean

Jerome Christensen

> *But the stranger has appeared, the forgiving friend has come, even the Son of God from heaven: and to as many as have faith in his name, I say — the debt is paid for you; — the satisfaction has been made.*
> — SAMUEL TAYLOR COLERIDGE, *Aids to Reflection*

When, during his defense of genius from the abuse of anonymous critics, Coleridge asks in the *Biographia Literaria*, "Has the poet no property in his works?" he wishes his question to be rhetorical. And it can uncritically be taken so. But if rhetoric succeeds when it turns wishes into acts, criticism works when it reacts, when it returns the wish in a different, if not finer, tone. One reaction to the *Biographia* is to suspect that the poet's title to his works is not wholly secure — and if the poet's property in *his* works, so the man of letters' property in his literary life. Far from closing an argument, Coleridge's rhetorical question wishes open room for more, critical questions.

What is property? is so nearly the same question as what is propriety? that for Coleridge the answer to one is involved in the solution of the other. The solution of both involves the question of meaning itself. Coleridge raises that question and proposes a partial answer when he offers as preliminary justification of his distinction between imagination and fancy the observation that "in all societies there exists an instinct of growth, a certain collective, unconscious good sense working progressively to desynonymize those words originally of the same meaning." The history of language is the elaboration — creative, discriminating — of meanings. That process is progressive, indeed meaningful, however, only because it is the expression of a "certain . . . unconscious good sense," the active aspect

From *Romanticism and Language.* © 1984 by Cornell University. Cornell University Press, 1984. Originally entitled "The Mind at Ocean: The Impropriety of Coleridge's Literary Life."

of what Coleridge calls "the reversionary wealth of the mother tongue." The mother tongue is the matrix of nativeness, an abiding source of essential propriety which ordains that the elaboration of senses never strays from the good sense with which the language has been originally endowed and by which its history is silently nourished. And, though unconscious, the mother tongue is no spendthrift. Desynonymization is not a blind largesse but a canny outlay: *reversionary* wealth. Perpetually owned by its source, language is a property whose history is a disbursement of wealth under the terms of an estate that reserves the right of the future possession of all profit. The discrimination of words, the multiplication of senses, always contributes in inevitable recourse to the increase of aboriginal sense; history refills the plenum. Hence it is that as the historical process of discrimination is ideally a reunification, so the conscious desynonymization of certain words such as *imagination* and *fancy* is complemented by the meaningful resynonymization of others: particularly and crucially, *property* and *propriety*, words that were, we are informed, incorporated under the single spelling *propriety* in the seventeenth century, the last age of true sovereignty in nation and self. By resynonymizing property and propriety, Coleridge hopes to restore that lapsed sovereignty, the absolute synonym of self-possession, and to secure thereby what he calls the "sacred distinction between things and persons." The synonymity of *propriety* and *property* disciplines the dissolution of synonyms within history and the *Biographia* to a benign, unifying, self-confirming teleology.

When Coleridge writes of Gray's "imitation" in "The Bard" of a passage in Shakespeare's *Merchant of Venice* that "all the propriety was lost in the transfer," his remark both suggests the impropriety of tampering with a great poet's property and epitomizes the *Biographia* as a whole, which attempts to return all propriety lost in various deplorable transfers to where it belongs. One explanation for the eccentric method of the philosophical criticism of the *Biographia* is that propriety cannot, without hazard, be neatly abstracted for analysis because propriety belongs to the man; to transfer propriety from the person to the arid discourse of the understanding would be to assist in the dispossession that reason and imagination would reverse. As for the critic, so for the critic's critic: what is at stake for Coleridge in the issue of propriety can be most decorously engaged by examining, if not the man himself, at least that place where the man clearly perceives the liability of poetic transfer, in Gray's "imitation" of Shakespeare.

In Chapter I of the *Biographia* Coleridge contrasts the inspiriting meditative verse of William Lisle Bowles with the dessicated Augustan poetry of "point," wherein "matter and diction seemed . . . characterized not so much by poetic thoughts as by thoughts *translated* into the language of poetry." As another example of the defect of poetic translation or transfer, Coleridge juxtaposes Shakespeare and Gray. The Shakespeare:

How like a younker or a prodigal
The scarfed bark puts from her native bay,
Hugg'd and embraced by the strumpet wind!
How like the prodigal doth she return,
With over-weather'd ribs and ragged sails,
Lean, rent and beggar'd by the strumpet wind!
(*Merchant of Venice*, II.vi.14–19)

The Gray:

Fair laughs the morn, and soft the zephyr blows
While proudly riding o'er the azure realm
In gallant trim the gilded vessel goes,
YOUTH at the prow and PLEASURE at the helm;
Regardless of the sweeping whirlwind's sway,
That hush'd in grim repose, expects its evening prey.
("The Bard," II.ii.71–76)

Certainly Shakespeare's diction is both concrete and perspicuous: not only is it appropriate to the station of Gratiano, the character who speaks the lines, but the words are uniformly strict in their reference, and, taken together, enrich the rhetorical structure of the passage. The basic trope is metonymy, here doubled: the ship stands metonymically for the tenor of the lover's (Lorenzo's) mind, and the ship in turn becomes the tenor for the metonym of the younker, or errant youth. Metonymy, a figure of incapable imagination, here directly tropes that incapacity as an overreaching desire, but a desire subdued by decorous diction and by the disciplined symmetry of the twin "how like's," which enforce by repetition a powerful statement of a coherent moral economy. From its glad venture out in the bedizened pride of its youthful passion to its sad return, "lean, rent, and beggar'd," the ship of desire follows an ordained course. Desire may be satisfied—enjoyed in the margin, as it were—but it is represented only in the moral symmetry of its fond aspiration and its inevitable ruin. The repetition of "the strumpet wind" at the end of each rhetorical unit reinforces desire's essentially ironic structure. Nevertheless, though passion dies, death is endowed with a life-giving meaning through its subsumption in a larger pattern that both maintains and ultimately transfigures the ironic economy of the figure itself. Although the voyage outward, the metonymic thrust onto strange seas, may end in catastrophe, the ship does, reassuringly, return to shore—as a "prodigal." That repeated reference to "prodigal" signals that this necessary pattern is not merely circular but typically circular, charting in small the great romantic myth of the ill-starred journey out and the redemptive voyage back.

The synecdochic relations of this passage to the play as a whole seem at first sight to reinforce the sense of its complete, even ultimate, propriety and attest to Coleridge's canny advertence in the selection. Although the ships are figurative in the immediate context (the speculative byplay of Gratiano and Salarino as they await the tardy Lorenzo beneath Jessica's window), the figure is literalized in the central action of the play, only to be troped once again. The pattern that Gratiano finds in love's ardent venture imitates the fate of Antonio's actual argosy, the merchant ships that he has pledged as surety for his loan from Shylock. Antonio's gilded frigates in turn represent both the passion for Bassiano that motivated the loan and his proud self-sufficiency in the exercise of that passion. Passion and pride are chastened in the report of the destruction of Antonio's ships and by his consequent inability to redeem his loan. The penalty to be inflicted with evident justice by Shylock, though horrible, would nonetheless be the logical result and concrete manifestation of a loss of self in reckless and unacknowledged desire that has already occurred. On this level of the play, the transcendent economy that subsumes the figure of the ship is especially evident, for it is the catastrophe suffered by Antonio that makes possible Portia's famous redemptive speech in which the economy of desire and the economy of justice are (optatively) canceled under the dispensation of mercy. That the literal catastrophe of Antonio's ships has actually the emblematic function of heralding this theophany becomes evident when, in the final scene, Antonio receives the news from Portia that the real ships, the ones that are the pretexts for the figurative transactions of the play, have survived the storms after all—a providential reward granted to the prodigal Antonio now safe within the enchanted grounds of Belmont.

Gray seems to exploit the same metonymy as Shakespeare. Not only is his figure structured by desire, but the metonymy also represents desire and its inevitable fate. Though it is clearer in Gray than in Shakespeare that the speaker is not talking about actual ships, it is less clear exactly what he is talking about. The context supplies the grim prophecy of an eventual humbling of pride and a general tone of doom, but it is difficult to understand what the figure adds in either specificity or intensity to effects already amply elaborated. The problem lies in the vagueness of the tenor. The "gilded vessel" evidently stands for something like a man's falsely proud aspiration, but beyond that point glossing becomes guessing. I would suggest, however, that the obscurity of the referent enhances rather than diminishes the effect of the figure: the lack that articulates the tenor reinforces the lack that structurally afflicts desire—the apparent subject of the figure as a whole. The plot of Gray's passage also differs strikingly from Shakespeare's: in Gray the ship does not and will not return to shore. Instead of desire being judged according to a stable economy that is, in turn, subsumed by a transcendent value, in Gray the frigate of passion fares toward an inevitable and total loss. The ship has certainly been lost to the whirlwind from the moment it left the harbor, doomed, perhaps, even at its gilding. As it breasts the waves in the laughing morn it is as though evening were already falling, as though the whirlwind were attracting not only space but time within its deadly sway. The figure divulges death at every turn. Coleridge's most specific stricture against the impropriety of Gray's diction, that he "preferred the original on the ground that in the imitation it depended wholly in the compositor's putting, or not putting, a *small Capital* both in this and in many other passages of the same poet whether the words should be personifications or mere abstracts," marks the peculiar fatality of the figure. His objection seems to refer to the impossibility of keeping "youth" and "pleasure" on the same level of abstraction or concreteness at the same time, a problem indicated rather than solved by Coleridge's own capitalization (or was it only his compositor's?). If "YOUTH" is read as the personification of the abstraction "youth," then the personification necessarily evokes the person himself, a youthful body on the prow. To personify pleasure in the same degree might give it dramatic attributes but would leave it vitally short of embodied form. Although "youth" and "pleasure" ship out on the same "gilded vessel," they cannot both occupy the same figurative space, an incompatibility owed to the poet's failure to assign either signifier a place of its own. The factitious stability imposed by the compositor cannot, as Coleridge testifies, efface a slippage between personification and abstraction that, read morally, violates "the sacred distinction between things and persons" that the *Biographia* aims to indemnify and that, read phenomenologically, imitates the deadly circulation of the whirlwind that holds the passage in its sway. The confusion of person with thing into "an amphibious something, made up, half of image, and half of abstract meaning" is the very vertiginous fatality of desire that Gray figures. His imitation of Shakespeare loses all propriety in the transfer, in part because it figures the ease with which propriety *can* be transferred. In Gray propriety acts as if it had no place of its own in language. Its vagrancy undermines the autonomy of the subject that Coleridge would have it ground.

Although I have identified what are, I think, the standards Coleridge applies in his judgment of Gray's impropriety, to understand Coleridge's hypopoetics we must go further and examine the process of judgment as well. In this case we need to pursue the problem of imitation past the criteria of good and bad, to ask in what way Gray's passage is an imitation of Shakespeare at all. The two passages do not notably resemble each other; indeed, according to Gray's most recent editor, no one except Coleridge ever proposed a homology between the two figures. Given Coleridge's thorough disapproval of the Gray, it is peculiar that he would elevate it with the term "imitation," which in the *Biographia* he invariably opposes to mechanical copying as an honorific of Platonic lineage. Imitation, he says, "consists either in the interfusion of the SAME throughout the radically DIFFERENT, or of the different throughout a base radically the same." By calling the Gray an imitation, Coleridge invites us to examine the way in which same and different convene in the relations of the two passages. In the absence of any evident verbal or structural correspondence we must join with the idealist and ask in what way Gray "Shakespearanizes" the Shakespeare, in what way the latter passage does "master the essence" of the former. I will not pretend that that question is innocent; it queries the *Biographia* into a predicament because for Coleridge the essence of the Shakespeare *is* its propriety, which is just what he misses in Gray. To retrieve the *Biographia* from the predicament of implicit contradiction means that we have to turn against the text in order to make sense of, if not master, it. To turn against Coleridge is to follow Coleridge, however, for the charm of Gray's "imitation" is that it encourages what Coleridge calls "the too exclusive attention" to certain truths which tempts the reader "to carry those truths beyond their proper limits." What makes the Gray both an imitation and the model of a bad imitation in the *Biographia* is that its association with the Shakespeare provokes an exclusive attention that discovers in the source a previously imperceptible and unsuspected impropriety that subverts the idea of the proper limits of truth.

Attention to the Shakespeare with an eye to its genetic powers brings within ken the genealogy of the figure within the play. The progenitor is a comment by Salarino to Antonio in the first scene. He replies to the merchant's puzzled confession of sadness by observing, "Your mind is tossing on the ocean" (I.i.8). Salarino and Salanio account for Antonio's dejection by characterizing what they conceive to be his proper concern for his fleet. Salarino fancies that, were he in Antonio's place, in his anxiety he would convert all actions and objects into signs of commercial success or failure, and he justifies his diagnosis of Antonio's mood by the demonstrated power of his fancy to transfigure all things into versions of one obsessive concern: "Shall I have the thought/To think on this, and shall I lack the thought/That such a thing bechanced would make me sad?" (I.i.36–38). The physical lack is supplemented by thought, which is, however, motivated by a desire constituted by a lack that lets sadness in. Antonio does not directly dispute that his mind is tossing on the ocean; he only demurs that his cargo is safe because his "ventures are not in one bottom trusted" (I.i.42) and therefore his merchandise does not make him sad. In reply, Salarino not only maintains his analysis, he extends it by exploiting the substitutive dynamics implicit in the initial trope: "Why, then you are in love" (I.i.46). Salarino good-naturedly accepts Antonio's denial only to reduce it wittily to the absurd and thereby to sharpen his original point: if there is any explanation for Antonio's sadness, it is that his mind is tossing on the ocean, abroad in the bottom of a ship or a lover or both. As Salarino elaborates it, the mind tossing on the ocean is a figure for the abstraction of a person into its objects, a symptom of what might be called a metonymic moodiness in which the mind is vulnerable to the fever of substitution. One impropriety will beget another: the impropriety of a self abstracted into its aspects produces the impropriety of one aspect substituting for another: lover for self, ships for self, lover for ships, ships for lover. Not only one's chattel but the soundness of one's soul is submitted to the caprice of ocean squalls.

The mental association developed between Bassanio and ships, between ships and life, is fully staged in the courtroom scene of act 4, in which Antonio's resigned acceptance of death presumes an interchangeability among loss of merchandise, loss of Bassanio, and loss of life. Antonio's inability to distinguish between things and persons makes him the perfect match for Shylock and a fit subject both for Portia's virtuosic movement through the scales of passion and power in the courtroom and her later pointed play with the ring that Bassanio, abetted by Antonio, has simultaneously overvalued and underesteemed. Portia's every action from act 4 on works to cut Bassanio away from his imaginative possession by Antonio — bloodless cuts that reduce Antonio as thoroughly as ever would have Shylock's crude, murderous violence. Portia reduces Antonio both by cutting him off from Bassanio, for whose sake he claims to love the world, and by restoring him to his ships, which she implicitly gives as sufficient compensation for the loss of his lover. Indeed, Antonio confirms the adequacy of the compensation when he gratefully exclaims, "Sweet lady, you have given me life and living" (V.i.286). Although the play has plotted the restoration of life before living, Antonio's conjunction of the two is true to their identification in his imagination. Returning the ships is returning Antonio to his life less than before, not because Bassanio has been cut loose but because the loss of Bassanio makes no essential difference. That Antonio's life and living must be returned to him by another character seals Antonio's impropriety. Portia's surgery confirms Salarino's diagnosis: Antonio less than before is Antonio the same as before: the merchant's mind still finds its life only in its movable property and tosses abroad in a confusion of persons and things.

That a mind can be constantly at sea is the concealed impropriety of a figure that may return the prodigal ship and depict Antonio's recovery from sadness but can efface neither the liability to prodigality nor the metonymic impulse that constitutes and disables Antonio's imagination. Nor, finally, can the return of the prodigal ships and the retreat into Belmont cancel the impropriety of Shakespeare's substitution of the figure for the man, which makes Antonio's attitudes and actions not only congruent with the figure of the ships' venture and return but apparently a function of the figure — a mechanism of transfer whose power implies a loss of the person's autonomy to something neither person nor thing. Gray's imitation is vicious because it accurately imitates the transfer of propriety that motivates the machine of Shakespeare's play.

Chronology

1564	William Shakespeare born at Stratford-on-Avon to John Shakespeare, a butcher, and Mary Arden. He is baptized on April 26.
1582	Marries Anne Hathaway in November.
1583	Daughter Susanna born, baptized on May 26.
1585	Twins Hamnet and Judith born, baptized on February 2.
1588–90	Sometime during these years, Shakespeare goes to London, without family.
1588–89	First plays are performed in London.
1590–92	*The Comedy of Errors*, the three parts of *Henry VI*.
1593–94	Publication of *Venus and Adonis* and *The Rape of Lucrece*, both dedicated to the Earl of Southampton. Shakespeare becomes a sharer in the Lord Chamberlain's company of actors. *The Taming of the Shrew, Two Gentlemen of Verona, Richard III*.
1595–97	*Romeo and Juliet, Richard II, King John, A Midsummer Night's Dream, Love's Labor's Lost*.
1596	Son Hamnet dies. Grant of arms to father.
1597	*The Merchant of Venice, Henry IV* (part 1). Purchases New Place in Stratford.
1598–1600	*Henry IV* (part 2), *As You Like It, Much Ado About Nothing, Twelfth Night, The Merry Wives of Windsor, Henry V*, and *Julius Caesar*. Moves his company to the new Globe Theatre.
1601	*Hamlet*. Shakespeare's father dies, buried on September 8.
1603	Death of Queen Elizabeth; James VI of Scotland becomes James I of England; Shakespeare's company becomes the King's Men.
1603–4	*All's Well That Ends Well, Measure for Measure, Othello*.
1605–6	*King Lear, Macbeth*.
1607	Marriage of daughter Susanna on June 5.
1607–8	*Timon of Athens, Antony and Cleopatra, Pericles*.
1608	Death of Shakespeare's mother. Buried on September 9.

1609   *Cymbeline*, publication of sonnets. Shakespeare's company purchases Blackfriars Theatre.

1610–11   *The Winter's Tale, The Tempest*. Shakespeare retires to Stratford.

1616   Marriage of daughter Judith on February 10. William Shakespeare dies at Stratford on April 23.

1623   Publication of the Folio edition of Shakespeare's plays.

Contributors

HAROLD BLOOM, Sterling Professor of the Humanities at Yale University, is the author of *The Anxiety of Influence, Poetry and Repression*, and many other volumes of literary criticism. His forthcoming study, *Freud: Transference and Authority*, attempts a full-scale reading of all of Freud's major writings. A MacArthur Prize Fellow, he is general editor of five series of literary criticism published by Chelsea House.

SIGMUND FREUD, moralist, psychoanalyst, poet-critic, was "creator of the darkest Western vision of fatherhood since the ancient Gnostics." He himself "has become a generic father figure in Western culture, a fate he would have resented." — H.B.

E. E. STOLL was Professor of English at the University of Minnesota. His books include *Shakespeare and Other Masters* and *Art and Artifice in Shakespeare*.

HAROLD C. GODDARD was head of the English Department at Swarthmore College from 1909 to 1946. He is remembered not only for *The Meaning of Shakespeare* but also for his writings on American Transcendentalism.

C. L. BARBER was Professor of Literature at the University of California at Santa Cruz. His best-known study is *Shakespeare's Festive Comedy*.

LESLIE A. FIEDLER is Professor of English at the State University of New York at Buffalo, and is a well-known fiction writer and essayist. His many books include *The Image of the Jew in American Fiction* and *Love and Death in the American Novel*.

RENE GIRARD is University Professor of the Humanities at Stanford University. His books include *Mensonge romantique et verité romanesque* (Deceit, Desire and the Novel) and *La violence et la sacre* (Violence and the Sacred).

MARC SHELL is Professor of English at the State University of New York at Buffalo. He is the author of *The Economy of Literature* and *Money, Language, and Thought: Literary and Philosophical Economies from the Medieval to the Modern Era*.

131

JEROME CHRISTENSEN is Professor of English at The Johns Hopkins University. His books include *Coleridge's Blessed Machine of Language*.

Bibliography

Alvis, John, and Thomas G. West, eds. *Shakespeare as Political Thinker*. Durham: Carolina Academic Press, 1981.

Auden, W. H. *The Dyer's Hand*. New York: Vintage Books, 1968.

Barnet, Sylvan, ed. *Twentieth-Century Interpretations of "The Merchant of Venice."* Englewood Cliffs, N.J.: Prentice-Hall, 1970.

Berry, Edward. *Shakespeare's Comic Rites*. Cambridge: Cambridge University Press, 1984.

Berry, Ralph. *Shakespeare's Comedies: Explorations in Form*. Princeton: Princeton University Press, 1972.

Bradbury, Malcolm, and David Palmer, eds. *Shakespearian Comedy*. London: Edward Arnold Publishers, 1972.

Brown, John Russell, and Bernard Harris, eds. *Early Shakespeare*. London: Edward Arnold Publishers, 1961.

Burckhardt, Sigurd. *Shakespearian Meanings*. Princeton: Princeton University Press, 1968.

Cohen, Walter. "*The Merchant of Venice* and the Possibilities of Historical Criticism." *ELH* 49 (1982): 765–89.

Danson, Lawrence. *The Harmonies of "The Merchant of Venice."* New Haven and London: Yale University Press, 1978.

Dawson, Anthony B. *Indirections: Shakespeare and the Art of Illusion*. Toronto: University of Toronto Press, 1978.

Elam, Keri. *Shakespeare's Universe of Discourse*. Cambridge: Cambridge University Press, 1984.

Evans, Bertrand. *Shakespeare's Comedies*. Oxford: Clarendon Press, 1960.

Garber, Marjorie. *Coming of Age in Shakespeare*. London: Methuen, 1981.

Goddard, Harold C. *The Meaning of Shakespeare*. Chicago: The University of Chicago Press, 1951.

Grebaner, Bernard. *The Truth About Shylock*. New York: Random House, 1962.

Greenblatt, Stephen. "Marlowe, Marx, and Anti-Semitism." *Critical Inquiry* 5 (1978): 291–308.

Hassel, R. Chris. *Faith and Folly in Shakespeare's Romantic Comedies.* Athens: University of Georgia Press, 1980.

Hibbard, G. R. *The Making of Shakespeare's Dramatic Poetry.* Toronto: University of Toronto Press, 1981.

Hill, R. F. "*The Merchant of Venice* and the Pattern of Romantic Comedy." *Shakespeare Survey* 28 (1975): 75–88.

Kirschbaum, Leo. *Character and Characterization in Shakespeare.* Detroit: Wayne State University Press, 1962.

Leggatt, Alexander. *Shakespeare's Comedy of Love.* London: Methuen, 1974.

MacCary, W. Thomas. *Friends and Lovers.* New York: Columbia University Press, 1985.

Moody, A. D. "Shakespeare: *The Merchant of Venice.*" *Studies in English Literature* 21 (1964).

Nevo, Ruth. *Comic Transformations in Shakespeare.* London and New York: Methuen, 1980.

Panitz, Esther. *The Alien in Their Midst: Images of Jews in English Literature.* London and Toronto: Associated University Presses, 1981.

Richmond, Hugh M. *Shakespeare's Sexual Comedy: A Mirror for Lovers.* Indianapolis and New York: Bobbs-Merrill, 1971.

Salinger, Leo. *Shakespeare and the Traditions of Comedy.* Cambridge: Cambridge University Press, 1974.

Schwartz, Murray, and Coppelia Kahn, eds. *Representing Shakespeare.* Baltimore: The Johns Hopkins University Press, 1980.

Sundelson, David. *Shakespearian Restorations of the Father.* New Brunswick, N.J.: Rutgers University Press, 1983.

Tillyard, E. M. W. *Shakespeare's Early Comedies.* London: Chatto and Windus, 1965.

Acknowledgments

"The Theme of the Three Caskets" by Sigmund Freud from *The Standard Edition of the Complete Psychological Works of Sigmund Freud* 12 (1911–1913), edited by James Strachey and Anna Freud, © 1958 by The Institute of Psycho-Analysis and Mrs. Alix Strachey. Reprinted by permission of Sigmund Freud Copyrights Ltd., The Institute of Psycho-Analysis, The Hogarth Press, and Basic Books, Inc.

"Shylock" by E. E. Stoll from *Shakespeare Studies: Historical and Comparative in Method* by E. E. Stoll, © 1927 by Macmillan Company, © 1941 by E. E. Stoll. Reprinted by permission.

"Portia's Failure" (originally entitled "*The Merchant of Venice*") by Harold C. Goddard from *The Meaning of Shakespeare* by Harold C. Goddard, © 1951 by The University of Chicago. Reprinted by permission of The University of Chicago Press.

"Wealth's Communion and an Intruder" (originally entitled "The Merchants and the Jew of Venice: Wealth's Communion and an Intruder") by C. L. Barber from *Shakespeare's Festive Comedy* by C. L. Barber, © 1959 by Princeton University Press. Reprinted by permission of Princeton University Press.

"These Be the Christian Husbands" (originally entitled "The Jew as Stranger: Or 'These be the Christian Husbands' ") by Leslie A. Fiedler from *The Stranger in Shakespeare* by Leslie A Fiedler, © 1972 by Leslie A. Fiedler. Reprinted by permission of Croom Helm Ltd. and the author.

"To Entrap the Wisest" (originally entitled " 'To Entrap the Wisest': A Reading of *The Merchant of Venice*") by René Girard from *Literature and Society — Selected Papers from The English Institute*, no. 3, edited by Edward W. Said, © 1980 by The English Institute. Reprinted by permission of The Johns Hopkins University Press.

135

"The Wether and the Ewe: Verbal Usury" (originally entitled "The Wether and the Ewe: Verbal Usury in *The Merchant of Venice*") by Marc Shell from *The Kenyon Review* 1, no. 4 (Fall 1979), © 1979 by Kenyon College. Reprinted by permission of the author and publisher. This essay also appears, in slightly altered form, in *Money, Language, and Thought* by Marc Shell (University of California Press, 1982).

"The Mind at Ocean" (originally entitled "The Mind at Ocean: The Impropriety of Coleridge's Literary Life") by Jerome Christensen from *Romanticism and Language*, edited by Arden Reed, © 1984 by Cornell University. Reprinted by permission of Cornell University Press.

Index